INTERNATIONAL PERSPECTIVES ON ORGANIZED CRIME

Jane Rae Buckwalter
Editor

INTERNATIONAL PERSPECTIVES ON ORGANIZED CRIME

Jane Rae Buckwalter
Editor

Office of International Criminal Justice
The University of Illinois at Chicago

Chicago, Illinois

International perspectives on organized crime / Jane Rae Buckwalter, editor.
p. cm.
Includes bibliographical references and index.
1. Organized crime--Congresses.I. Buckwalter, Jane.

HV6441.I65 1990   90-44817364.1'06--dc20CIP

Copyright 1990 by the Office of International Criminal Justice
The University of Illinois at Chicago
1333 South Wabash Avenue
Box 53, Chicago, Illinois 60605

ISBN: 0-942511-41-7 (Paperback)
ISBN: 0-942511-42-5 (Cloth)

LOC: 90-62691

Production Manager: *Tonya M. Matz*
Production Assistant: *Erika Maybon*
Book Cover: *Jerzy J. Hoga*

ACKNOWLEDGEMENTS

As editor of this publication, I wish to express a special note of appreciation to those people who made the volume possible. First, of course, the authors who prepared thoughtful presentations and allowed their work to be included. Next, members of the OICJ staff, in particular, Tonya Matz, Erika Maybon and Mr. Adam Liu, played significant roles in bringing this book into print. Finally, the fine editorial skills of Susan Flood were invaluable in refining and completing this book.

Jane Rae Buckwalter
Editor

Table of Contents

FOREWORD

The willingness of individuals to obtain an unfair advantage over others by means of violence and deceit, in a way that is clearly outside of accepted societal norms, continues to be part and parcel of the human experience. Illicit association and organization for the purpose of profiting from criminal activity has existed since time immemorial and will continue to threaten social institutions.

The ability of organized criminals to subvert judicial systems, corrupt social institutions and intimidate governments is clearly evident in Latin America, Asia, Africa and the Middle East. Demographic trends throughout the world augur a period where criminal activity will be a more pervasive and grave problem than at any other time in recent history. These demographic trends include explosive growth in some of the world's densest urban centers, an increased flow of refugees from third world conflicts, a lower level of education and, perhaps most worrisome, a decline in living standards and increase of poverty in many less developed countries and among broad population segments in industrialized nations.

The Office of International Criminal Justice (OICJ) at the University of Illinois at Chicago (UIC) sponsors annual conferences whose objective is to research and analyze issues of critical concern to the international criminal justice community. OICJ and its cosponsors organize these conferences and publish the proceedings as a means of contributing valuable insights to law enforcement policy makers, criminal justice practitioners and others. Additionally OICJ seeks to provide significant information that will enhance society's ability to meet the challenges of the future.

The fourth annual conference, which focused on the problems of organized crime and terrorism, involved over 200 professional law enforcement officers, scholars and government officials from 23 countries, including the Soviet Union. The presentations collected in this volume offer a unique opportunity to gain an appreciation of the international dimensions of the problem posed by organized crime.

Rodrigo Paris Steffens, a member of the Crime Prevention and Criminal Justice Branch of the United Nations in Vienna, emphasized that although the United Nations Congress on Crime Prevention and Criminal Justice is almost as old as the UN, it had given minimal share of attention to the problem of organized crime. However, the explosive growth of organized criminal activities since World War II has reached such dimensions that it is "threatening basic social and political institutions, and in many cases, for all practical purposes, replacing governments of some nations."

Further elaborating on the evolving sophistication of organized crime, both Donald Lavey, a special agent with the Federal Bureau of Investigation, (currently assigned to INTERPOL as Chief of the International Anti-Terrorism Unit) and Matt L. Rodriguez, deputy superintendent of the Police Department of Chicago, Illinois, independently concluded that as the operations of criminal groups became more sophisticated, their members are developing significant managerial skills, such as detailing job assignments, ensuring operational security, enforcing discipline and developing and maintaining successful relationships with unethical professionals, who provide consulting services.

As a consequence criminal organizations are developing the organizational sophistication, the economies of scale, the monopolistic advance of market share and the improvement of resources that will ensure future growth in other criminal areas as well as in legitimate enterprises. Competition is eliminated by any means possible, including violence. The long-term strategy of such groups is to expand market control and facilitate business activities by corrupting institutions, public officials and private citizens.

The rule of survival of the fittest applies to criminal enterprises. Society is not threatened by the isolated activities of amateurs and freelancers, but rather by those organizations that have survived. These are the organizations that law enforcement must neutralize if it is to succeed in its efforts to control organized crime. But these are also the same organizations whose material, financial and human resources often exceed those available to law enforcement. Law enforcement efforts are complicated by the ability of organized criminal gangs to use their considerable resources, power and influence to insulate and protect their hierarchy from discovery and prosecution.

Judith F. Dobkin, a prosecutor with the U.S. Department of Justice's Organized Crime and Racketeering Section, outlined legitimate business areas, such as labor organizations and transportation, where organized crime has made significant inroads.

Popular support of organized crime figures and widespread disregard for statutes outlawing particular modes of behavior, such as prostitution and narcotics usage, also obstructs law enforcement efforts. Law enforcement officials readily acknowledge that organized crime exists because substantial segments of the population demand illicit services. In the United States, during 1988, approximately 28 million people used an illegal drug and 14.5 million, or approximately one in twenty, used illegal drugs during the month prior to the survey. These statistics, with some variation, are comparable to those of other industrialized nations. An even larger portion of the population tacitly condones illegal activity. Public apathy and glamorous portraits of legendary criminals in literature, television and movies pose considerable obstacles to police investigations and weaken popular and political support for law enforcement efforts against organized crime.

In lower income neighborhoods, from Moscow to Rio de Janeiro, New York to Pretoria, successful criminals are admired, respected and emulated by poor youths. Organized gangs deliberately cultivate this image and large sums of money are used to intimidate and motivate.

All the speakers recognized the importance of international cooperation. Dr. Aldo Grassi, presiding judge in some of Italy's most important organized crime trials, underlined a significant concept: "The fact that individuals are subject to the authority of the State to which they belong means that international law is generally directed toward countries and not individual citizens. International law regulations require the State to punish citizens for committing crimes of an international nature over which they have jurisdiction."

The participants in the OICJ Organized Crime and Terrorism conference unanimously agreed that the colloquium represented a valuable opportunity to develop productive professional relationships on an international scale and to acquire a significant understanding of how other countries handle operational and investigative problems in the criminal justice field.

The full text of the presentations made by the panel of experts follows. The Office of International Criminal Justice believes that this publication represents a significant and lasting contribution to the understanding of the international aspects of organized crime and will provide the basis for future research by students and practitioners in the field of criminal justice.

James R. Sutton
Director, Office of Security Programs
University of Illinois at Chicago
December 1990

CONTROLLING ORGANIZED CRIME IN CANADA

Rodney T. Stamler

LAUNDERING PROCEEDS OF CRIME

Bill C-61, effective January 1, 1989, allows Canada to take action to trace, freeze, seize and forfeit the proceeds of enterprise crime under criminal laws. Through amendments to the Criminal Code, the Narcotic Control Act and Food and Drugs Act, a new offense of Laundering Proceeds was added. In addition, court orders to seize, freeze or restrain property believed to be the proceeds of enterprise crime are available through application to a Supreme or Superior Court Judge. Such proceeds may subsequently be ordered forfeited following the conviction for a related enterprise crime or following a forfeiture hearing in the event the accused person has absconded.

This new law provides a remedy, where none previously existed, to restrain intangible property (such as a bank account) or immovable property (such as real estate) when it is established that such property is believed to be the proceeds of an enterprise crime. The new laws permit the seizure and forfeiture of all classes of property obtained from enterprise crime. This indeed constitutes an effective weapon in the continuing effort by law enforcement to dismantle powerful criminal organizations.

ENTERPRISE CRIME

Businessmen and other investors are attracted to commercial transactions and investments which produce the highest profit with the lowest risk. Criminals who engage in crime for financial gain are also attracted by high income and seek out crimes which produce the highest profit with the least risk. As in legitimate business and industry, the more profit that is generated, the larger and more complex the corporate structure or organization becomes. For this reason, high profit crime, or what has been defined as enterprise crime, attracts criminals; and if those criminals are successful, a criminal organization will likely result.

1

ORGANIZED CRIME

Whenever a criminal organization becomes established like a corporation, it takes on a life of its own. It can survive and continue even though some of the top level members leave or are imprisoned, providing the financial assets of the organization remain intact or the opportunity to make profits continues. There are currently several crime bosses who are serving prison terms, yet these persons are still in control of their empires and are producing profits from ongoing ventures.

Canada has major organized crime syndicates operating in every large metropolitan center in the country. These crime syndicates produce a cash flow from criminal enterprises which is estimated to be in excess of $10 billion annually. These funds, produced from a wide variety of criminal activity, are virtually tax free in the hands of the members of the crime syndicate. Bribes, pay-offs and kickbacks to corrupt public officials are only a few of the costs that crime groups must pay to maintain their enterprise crime activity. Most of the profits are laundered and then reinvested into legal or quasi-legal business ventures. This process, in turn, provides a shield of respectability to the top syndicate bosses.

For the top organized criminals, who seldom come into contact with the illegal activity, the risk of either losing the proceeds or being prosecuted for the substantive enterprise crime itself has been extremely low.

An established organized crime network usually adopts additional means of protecting itself. Crimes of violence such as serious assaults, property damage and homicides are included in the lexicon of organized crime activities. These violent acts are generally contracted out to specialized crime groups who are highly paid to produce certain results. The purpose may be to intimidate the public or individuals, to eliminate witnesses or informants, to acquire or secure territory or to enforce directives or rules on customers and group members.

These contracts for violent acts or murder are often carried out on a national or international basis. With no visible evidence or motive and no witnesses to establish any contact between the victim and the criminal, the crime again falls into a low-risk enterprise crime for both crime groups involved.

MONEY LAUNDERING

One of the few connecting links between the substantive enterprise crime, the bribe or kickback or the contract murder is the flow of money or other assets used to make the payment. For this reason, successful or major organized crime groups use sophisticated money transfer systems to ensure that there are no links between a crime boss and a street criminal. These systems are generally referred to as money laundering schemes.

Laundering schemes used to move illegally obtained funds vary widely and are as complex as legitimate business and commercial transactions. Through a variety of ways, cash can be secretly transferred anywhere in the world. This includes the use of corporations, business entities or phony business contracts, all carried out under the guise of a legitimate business enterprise.

As criminal organizations are formed to specialize in contract murder and violent acts intended to intimidate, so criminal organizations are formed to specialize in money laundering. Meyer Lansky was the first to perfect money laundering for Mafia families during the post-war era in the United States. Lansky's money laundering operations extended into Canada as well. One of Lansky's specialties was operating gambling casinos. Cuba and the Bahamas were his first ventures, and he used these locations to launder money for North American criminals. His Canadian connections in the money laundering business were Louis Chesler and businessman John Pullman, both of Toronto. Tax havens such as Switzerland, Grand Cayman and the Bahamas were used extensively by the trio, and millions of dollars were laundered for organized crime.

The Quebec Crime Commission found that one Montreal resident named William O'Bront operated a money laundering service in that city for several Canadian organized crime groups. O'Bront used at least 14 business corporations and 46 people to launder money for 32 organized crime figures. Over a period of several years he is known to have laundered more than $84 million. The Commission found that he was only one of many money launderers in Montreal during that same period of time. All were used to clean proceeds from criminal activity.

In one case a business was used to give the appearance that funds from a marijuana distribution network were income from retail furniture sales; the proceeds of drug trafficking were deposited daily in the firm's bank account. Although this method will likely attract various types of tax payments, it is extremely difficult to identify the unlawful money flow.

TAX HAVENS

Many countries present themselves as tax havens where bank and corporate secrecy laws are strictly enforced. Countries such as Panama, the Bahamas, Switzerland, Luxembourg, the Channel Islands, Hong Kong, Vanatu and many others are providing criminals with a full range of financial services. These include secret numbered bank accounts, beneficially held corporations and secret trusts along with a full range of services performed by lawyers, accountants and investment dealers.

A number of different types of institutions are used to transfer funds from Canada to tax havens. These include:

- Canadian banks with international branches or facilities
- Trust companies and provincial banking institutions
- Shipping companies
- Real estate companies
- Travel agencies
- Money changers
- Insurance companies
- Finance companies
- Brokerage and investment companies
- International trading companies
- Holding companies
- Multinational corporations

Although unlawful laundering schemes are as varied and complex as legitimate business transactions, there are several commonly known procedures to move illegal funds out of the country.

Canadian Banks

Canadian banks operate international departments and foreign subsidiaries in most of the tax havens. Through a variety of banking procedures, cash deposited in Canada can be transferred anywhere in the world. The actual transfer may involve the issuance of a bank cheque or order or by simply electronically crediting an account abroad. The advantages of using this system are that it seldom attracts attention and is not easily identified as part of an unlawful scheme. The disadvantage is that if Canadian law enforcement authorities detect the unlawful acts and follow the transactions to the bank, records in Canada will provide evidence of the transactions. This method, however, can be further protected by criminals if they are able to bribe bank officials

4

who may be in a position to make tracing of the funds through the bank almost impossible.

In addition to established chartered banks operating in Canada, there are a number of foreign banks or "B" banks performing a parallel banking service. As well, there are hundreds of agents of foreign banks who operate in Canada in a semi-clandestine manner. They are able to provide consulting services and arrange or facilitate the movement of money from Canada to a bank in a foreign jurisdiction.

A laundering system used by a Montreal heroin trafficking organization involved the purchase of more than $30 million in bank drafts with proceeds from illegal heroin sales over a two-year period. The bank drafts were purchased with cash totalling up to $30,000 on each occasion and were delivered to a bank in Switzerland. A bank employee who was aware of the illegal nature of the funds assisted in the transaction.

Money Exchanges

Businesses and financial institutions involved in the exchange of money have been known to accept large amounts of cash, thus facilitating a laundering system. Using a corporation as a front, the criminal can engage a foreign lawyer or business agent to represent his interest in a country where his corporation also has status. He then makes a large cash transfer to his corporation through the money exchange. The foreign bank will accommodate the money exchange entity in the transfer, because they frequently have legitimate business dealings with each other.

Brokerage Houses

Brokerage houses have been used to transfer large quantities of cash. Understandably, if they believe they are executing orders for a potentially important client or respected customer of a foreign bank, they will be more than willing to provide this service. One scheme involves a foreign bank that unknowingly represents a criminal and places an order with a Canadian broker for a large sum in securities. The bank advises the broker that the funds will be paid directly in Canada through a courier. The criminal then engages a courier who delivers the funds, in whatever form, and the securities are sent to the foreign bank, where they are later recovered by the criminal.

Travel Agencies

Travel agencies with multinational connections have become involved in the movement of funds. These agencies are primarily involved in the laundering business and charge fees to move currency from one country to another, but such fees are not significant enough to deter the criminal. Because of the nature of their business, they can arrange to transfer large sums of cash directly to another country where they have an affiliated office. There the money can usually be changed into foreign currency and moved onward by simply using the banking system. The travel agency may or may not be aware of the true purpose of the transaction.

Couriers

The simplest and safest way to move cash is to carry the funds to a foreign country. The most common procedure is to engage a courier to transport the money out of the country in a suitcase, briefcase or money belt. This system leaves no paper trail within Canada. There are a number of routes that couriers can take when moving money, although the most popular is by air to the Caribbean Islands or Bermuda. European countries are also used, in particular Switzerland, Liechtenstein and Monaco. Money couriers are usually lawyers, accountants or businessmen who may operate a money laundering service for a fixed fee. Some are agents or even salaried employees of Swiss and Caribbean banks. Agents and employees are located in many of the major cities of Canada.

SERVICES PROVIDED IN TAX HAVEN COUNTRIES

Financial Institutions

In addition to the usual banking services, many banks in tax haven countries provide secret numbered accounts where the names of the depositors are held separate from the accounts themselves. The name may be held by a separate entity such as a trust company affiliated with the bank. Where a banking facility comprises several corporate entities, the name of the depositor may be held by one corporation, the actual bank account with another and an investment certificate issued by another. This type of banking system makes it difficult for foreign courts or law enforcement agencies to identify money flow within one institution.

Offshore Corporations

Most tax havens in the Caribbean and Europe have a system providing for the incorporation of business and holding entities that will provide a high degree of anonymity to the beneficial owner. These corporations are permitted to carry on business transactions both within and outside the country. The corporation may be managed by a resident business agent, who is shown as the resident officer of the corporation. The names of the local lawyers who incorporate the company remain as the officers and directors on the corporate records. The true and beneficial owner will usually be named in the records of a government department or agency and these are kept secret by law, making it very difficult for foreign courts and officials to penetrate. The corporation may carry out banking transactions and be the owner of secret numbered accounts, both within the jurisdiction and in other tax-free areas.

One money launderer who worked exclusively for a drug trafficking organization testified that to launder the proceeds he used a business incorporated in the Cayman Islands which, in turn, had an account in a bank in the Bahamas. This system was used to ensure that his name did not appear at the Bahamian bank, where the proceeds were being held on deposit. The Grand Cayman company was managed by a local solicitor and the launderer's name was not listed on the corporate records.

Resident Agents and Business Managers

These are generally accountants or businessmen who act as managers of corporations for the beneficial owners. Laws generally provide for maximum protection for the beneficial owner. The agents or managers carry out banking and business transactions for the corporations.

Lawyers

Lawyers in tax havens can be engaged by foreign criminals to incorporate businesses or holding companies and to be named as directors and officers. These corporations are allowed to operate tax free and with maximum security under the law. Lawyers are generally forbidden under their domestic law, in addition to the usual solicitor-client privilege, to divulge the names of the beneficial owners of the corporations. Generally, citizens of tax havens are not permitted to directly use the facilities of this class of corporation. It is clear that these services are intended only for foreigners who are likely to invest large sums of money and wish anonymity and protection.

REPATRIATION OF THE LAUNDERED FUNDS

After money has safely reached the tax haven and is deposited in a bank in the name of a beneficially owned corporation by means of one of the schemes previously outlined, only part of the laundering cycle has been completed. The next stage involves the return of the funds in such a way that it appears that the funds were legitimately acquired by the criminal. Some of the procedures for repatriations which have been identified include:

Loan-Back Technique

A person with laundered money in a tax haven bank now decides that he requires the use of what would appear to be legitimate funds in Canada. The first step of the "loan-back" method is to arrange the purchase of a Canadian investment by making a small down payment with "clean money." The person then arranges to borrow the balance of the purchase price from his tax haven enterprise, which may be one of his offshore corporations. The individual then repays the loan as if it were a legitimate arms-length transaction. In this way, he not only repatriates his money, he pays himself interest, which is deductible for Canadian tax purposes. Once this loan is repaid, he can continue to lend himself more funds to acquire legitimate assets.

This transaction rarely occurs directly with the foreign bank where the money is deposited, but usually through one or more offshore corporations. For example, money in a Swiss bank may first go to the criminal's Liechtenstein corporation which transfers the money to his Bahamian corporation which, in turn, makes the money available to a Canadian lawyer who makes the funds available to the criminal in Canada. His Bahamian offshore corporation may be a trust and loan company or an insurance company, making the transaction look even more legitimate.

Direct Investment

Instead of using a loan-back method, a criminal may make the investment using his foreign offshore company as the front. Legitimate businesses may accept the criminal as a "partner." The "partner" then makes his investment using the laundered funds, via his foreign country.

Purchasing One's Own Property

By using laundered funds from a foreign bank, the criminal purchases his own property or business at a highly inflated price, and then repatriates more funds to Canada.

Double Invoicing

Once the criminal has become established in a quasi-legitimate business in Canada, he can use this entity to facilitate the laundering of funds through a variety of ways. Some of the more common systems include double invoicing, by overpricing the goods or property which are the subject of the transaction. For example, a Canadian business purchases property at an artificially high price from its related foreign company. The difference between the artificial price and the real or actual price is deposited in the bank account of the foreign subsidiary company in one of the tax havens. A reverse situation involves the Canadian entity selling the property at an artificially low price. The difference is eventually deposited in the same type of bank.

CONCLUSION

Canadian-based criminal syndicates and major enterprise criminals have developed many laundering schemes that fully exploit the facilities provided by the tax haven countries. The cash flow through the complexities of financial laundering is difficult enough to track but when it becomes further complicated by restrictive foreign laws and inadequate investigative procedure, it becomes virtually impossible to penetrate a carefully designed international money laundering scheme. Yet, it remains imperative to obtain all the evidence to be found in a laundering scheme because it helps identify the member of the conspiracy or syndicate and helps prove the full extent of criminal activity.

For their part, the tax haven countries must protect their banking system and the names of their clients in their competition for foreign investment, and hence, the survival of an important part of their economy. Tax havens, therefore, will generally refuse to cooperate, unless it can be shown that to do so would make them appear to harbour criminals.

On December 20, 1988, a United Nations Conference in Vienna adopted a new convention against Illicit Traffic in Narcotic Drugs and Psychotropic Substances. This new convention calls on member states, who become parties, to adopt measures in their criminal laws to identify, trace, freeze or seize and confiscate property that is the proceeds of drug trafficking. In addition, the convention requires parties to adopt criminal laws to make it an offense to possess or launder the proceeds of drug trafficking within their territory whether the substantive offense of drug trafficking was committed within their territory or not.

The convention also requires that the state parties ensure that courts and competent authorities look more seriously at offenses relating to such crimes as drug money laundering when an offender belongs to an organized crime group or is involved in international organized criminal activities.

In agreeing to adopt the provisions of this convention, the conference members stated that they were aware that illicit traffic of drugs generates large financial profits and wealth, enabling transnational criminal organizations to penetrate, contaminate and corrupt the structures of government, legitimate commercial and financial business and society at all levels. The convention notes that the member states attending the conference were determined to deprive persons engaged in illicit traffic of drugs of the proceeds of their criminal activities and thereby eliminate their main incentive for so doing.

Canada has clearly remained in step with the attitudes expressed by member states of the United Nations by amending its Criminal Laws and adopting the provisions of Bill C-61. It now remains for Canadian law enforcement, attorneys general, crown prosecutors as well as the victims of enterprise crime to use and develop this law before the courts, to make it as effective as possible in curbing the financial profits of organized enterprise criminals.

While the new laws in Canada will not immediately solve the problems of obtaining evidence and identifying proceeds in tax-haven countries, the new provisions of the Criminal Code will provide authority to deal more effectively with repatriated property which has been returned to Canada.

Through the use of net worth investigations and evidence, it may be possible to establish that a person has knowingly benefited from the proceeds of enterprise crime, even though the original funds have taken a circuitous route, through offshore banks and corporations, before final investment or use in Canada.

The law also provides some remedy to identify and forfeit proceeds that have been derived from enterprise type crimes in other countries where such proceeds have been laundered for investment in Canada.

RODNEY T. STAMLER

Rodney Stamler joined the Royal Canadian Mounted Police (RCMP) in 1956. He served as a Detective Inspector in the Commercial Crime Branch of the RCMP; as District Commander for the Southern Western Ontario Region; and as Officer in Charge of the Commercial Crime Branch at RCMP Headquarters in Ottawa. In 1980, he assumed the appointment as Director of Drug Enforcement. He was also appointed to the United Nations Division of Narcotic Drugs in Vienna to assist in the development of an international agreement to seize and forfeit the proceeds of drug trafficking. In July 1986, Mr. Stamler was elected chairman of the Main Committee of the First United Nations Drug Law Enforcement Conference in Vienna, where 115 countries participated. After 33 years of service, he retired with the rank of Assistant Commissioner in 1989. He has authored numerous articles in national and international publications, including the United Nations Bulletin on Narcotic Drugs. Mr. Stamler is now a partner at Peat Marwick, Lindquist and Holmes, forensic accounting division, in Toronto.

THE ROLE OF THE UNITED NATIONS IN COMBATING ORGANIZED CRIME

Rodrigo Paris-Steffens

The United Nations Congress on Crime Prevention and Criminal Justice is almost as old as the United Nations itself. But until now, it has given only a minimal share of attention to the phenomenon of organized crime. This apparent neglect has its origin in two factors.

First, throughout the early decades of the program, the emphasis was on a narrower conception of human rights. The program was mainly addressed to extending human rights protections to adult and juvenile offenders. This resulted in the adoption of international guidelines by previous United Nations Congresses on the Prevention of Crime and the Treatment of Offenders. These guidelines covered areas such as the standard minimum rules for the treatment of prisoners, the standard minimum rules for the behavior of law enforcement officers or, more recently, the standard minimum rules for the administration of juvenile justice.

The second factor was that, rightly or wrongly, organized crime was perceived until relatively recently as basically a domestic phenomenon limited to a few industrialized or even highly industrialized nations. In short, this meant that when one said "organized crime," the first place that came to mind was Chicago. The second place that came to mind was the United States. One was vaguely aware of the existence of some kind of a Sicilian connection, but the association with the United States predominated, partly as a reflection of reality, but also as a result of a successful movie industry that inundated the public with images of Scarface, Dillinger, Al Capone and others.

These two factors have undergone considerable change in the recent past. First the conception of human rights has become gradually broader, particularly with the inclusion of the idea of the human rights of the victim, specifically the victim of crime. This of course has led to a change in emphasis by the United Nations. The Seventh Congress, which took place in 1985 in Milan, Italy, adopted basic principles for the protection of victims. It is expected that the adoption of these first guidelines and principles will lead to the development of an international convention on the protection of victims.

Together with the change in our conception of human rights came a gradual internationalization of the organized crime phenomenon. What is meant by gradual internationalization? From the beginning, whenever two or more individuals got together to commit a crime or a series of crimes, some kind of division of labor occurred within the group. Therefore, one could talk about organized crime from the beginning of history and would be justified in saying that, leaving aside the loner, all crime has been in one sense or the other organized crime.

This phenomenon became more international and drug trafficking became more important and more menacing, threatening basic social and political institutions, and in many cases, for all practical purposes, replacing the governments of some nations. And as the business became more productive, the international community became more alarmed by the threat that this development represented.

This situation was already reflected at the Seventh Congress in 1985 in the unanimous adoption of two resolutions and the so-called Milan plan of action. The first resolution calls upon countries to rearrange their international agreements, to adopt new legislation and to facilitate in all possible ways a more effective international cooperation that could lead to control of this phenomenon. The second resolution addresses international drug trafficking; it calls upon member states to enter into bi-lateral or multi-lateral agreements regarding extradition, mutual judicial assistance and transfer of criminal proceedings, among other issues. The Milan plan of action addresses the need for international cooperation for effective action against organized crime and terrorism. These form the basis for an item on the agenda of the Eighth Congress that includes both organized crime and terrorism.

It is important, however, to avoid equating organized crime with drug trafficking. Illegal markets will exist for whatever illegal goods are in demand. Were we to succeed within the next five or 10 years in controlling drug trafficking, there is little doubt that organized crime would immediately find some other source of profit. There is already a white slave market in the world, and there are some indications that a black market for transplant organs could also develop as a profitable operation. Thus, although drug trafficking has given the United Nations an enormous impulse in this area, it is important to remember that organized crime does not deal exclusively with illegal drug trafficking.

The term organized crime may be a misnomer, in the same sense that talking about transnational cooperation would be a misnomer. We are not talking about a unitary phenomenon; we are talking about an interconnectedness of more or less organized criminal groups across national borders. It might have been better to talk about criminal

14

organizations rather than organized crime, because the term "organized crime" gives the idea of a unity that in reality does not exist. But apparently the term is here to stay.

How can organized crime be explained? Organized crime is not a new phenomenon, but modern organized crime must be understood as an expression of industrial society, in terms of the development of world commerce to levels never known before and of rapid transportation and instant worldwide communication. These technological advances facilitate both licit commercial and trade activities and the illicit organization or exploitation of illegal markets.

Another factor which should be taken into account is the need for organized crime to find the rule of law in at least some of the societies where it functions. Totalitarian systems, in which the rule of law does not exist, are not fruitful grounds for the development of organized crime. At least some of the societies being exploited have to be characterized by a juridical system in which even the criminal is protected, or perhaps in which the criminal is more protected than the non-criminal.

This is the current situation. Before explaining the role of the United Nations, it is important to dispel some possible misunderstandings. The United Nations includes two fundamentally different institutions. On the one hand the United Nations is the 159 member states and it reflects certain decision-making functions taking place at the level of the General Assembly and of the economic and social council. The United Nations is also the U.N. Secretariat, which includes a variety of units in charge of different topics, such as the U.N. Environment Program, the Division of Narcotic Drugs and the Crime Prevention and Criminal Justice branch. The Secretariat comprises those people who implement the decisions and policies of the majority of member states.

What is the United Nations' role? First, it can only take place within the legislative authority granted by the member states. It can serve, and is already serving, as an important international forum for the exchange of information and for the adoption of guidelines concerning crime prevention and criminal justice. For the next Congress, several instruments will be examined and possibly adopted: a draft model treaty on mutual assistance on judicial matters, a draft model treaty on extradition and basic guidelines for the transfer of criminal proceedings. All these will be examined by the Congress and hopefully adopted.

Just as organized crime could not exist without international cooperation, the only possibility of combating contemporary organized crime is through international cooperation. This cooperation is hampered by some predominant ideas that have been part of international order since it emerged over 200 years ago. One is the concept of sovereignty, and closely tied to it, the concept of territorial jurisdiction. These create a juridical no-man's land between non-overlapping jurisdictions, a fertile ground for organized crime where international criminality may flourish with impunity. The only way to establish the necessary international cooperation is by revising these antiquated concepts of sovereignty and jurisdiction. In a modern context, they are inadequate and they impede the proper functioning of international cooperation.

The congresses can bring together government representatives who through a long preparatory process, can present to the congresses guidelines and instruments ready for adoption which, it is hoped, will eventually take the form of conventions. For example, at the Ninth Congress in 1995, it is hoped that instead of having merely draft model treaties for mutual assistance, it will be possible to adopt an international convention on mutual assistance in judicial matters. This may sound like an extremely utopian vision but this is a general area in which the United Nations is and can be very instrumental.

Another area is technical assistance. The fact is that many countries do not possess either the resources or the expertise to engage in effective international cooperation. Many countries cannot establish electronic communications, or have little control of their internal situation. Without electronic networks for the exchange of information international cooperation is impossible because the escape routes will be too numerous. The only way to close those routes is through international cooperation and technical assistance to those countries, both in terms of training and equipment, and in terms of advisory services in order to help them change or adopt the necessary legislation.

These, then, are a few possible roles the United Nations can play in the fight against organized crime. But all this must be understood with the proviso that the U.N. can only do what member states permit, and only to the extent that member states are willing to pick up the bill. Without resources and without mandates, none of this will ever come true.

RODRIGO PARIS-STEFFENS

Mr. Paris-Steffens has been with the Crime Prevention and Criminal Justice Branch of the United Nations in Vienna since 1982. He was the Permanent Representative of Costa Rica to the U.N. in Vienna from 1980-1982. He was a member of the Costa Rican Delegation to the United Nations in New York from 1970-1974. He has a Ph.D. in sociology and has taught at Boston University, Vassar College and the University of Vienna.

POLICE POLICY IN DEALING WITH ORGANIZED CRIME

Matt L. Rodriguez

The major drug phenomena being experienced in the United States is a problem that beleaguers this country, but its scope is international. The recent historical perspective can be summarized by understanding that the "War On Crime," dating back to the administration of Lyndon Johnson, included a focus on drugs; in recent administrations the "War On Drugs" includes a focus on crime.

Drugs, the suppliers and the users represent a typical product supply and demand market. It is an illicit market because the people choose it to be so. The demand and value given the drugs are so great, however, that certain normal market forces are magnified and accelerated. They include development of criminal apparatus for acquisition, distribution and sale; sophistication of criminal organizations; continued drive for greater share of the market; and the tendency for "survival of the fittest."

Economics and marketing, however, are not the focus of this paper. The idea is rather to compare this isolated period, the drug era, with a relatively recent period called Prohibition. Many of the basic circumstances are strikingly similar. The Prohibition era provided the impetus, organizational sophistication and resources for the resulting phenomenon called traditional organized crime. The market forces then created circumstances that allowed for the emergence of a distinctive criminal group into a sophisticated organization that has survived for over five decades, becoming as significant an economic force as many corporate giants of this great country.

Today, there is no shortage of suggestions on how to solve the problem of the drugs. They range from studies concluding that legalization is an appropriate alternative, to an August 7, 1989, *Newsweek* article by Professor Richard Moran calling for the Mafia's return to the control of the drug trade, in order to establish peace, arbitrate disputes, set rules, and enforce discipline, thereby reducing the random street violence that is the hallmark of the drug gangs currently vying for their share of America's illegal drug market.

Too often, combatants in any battle can only see and are only interested in their field of conflict. There is the direct view of drug peddlers and their suppliers, the view of interdictions and supply sources and the view of money laundering apparatus. Hopefully, the

19

best strategists have a good conceptual perspective of this entire spectrum.

It is good practice to take a step back, to look at where we have been, where we are, and to look at where we are headed. That we can learn from the past, and in fact must learn from the past or be doomed to relive it, as warned by Santayana, is appropriate advice for law enforcement.

An "indirect phenomenon" may emerge from the drug era. Traditional organized crime was also an "indirect phenomenon" that emerged from the Prohibition era and spread like a cancer throughout this country. As with the current drug problem, during the Prohibition era there were presidential statements, border interdictions, property seizures, limited armed forces involvement and countless local arrests. Unfortunately, however, during Prohibition law enforcement targeted specific offenses and failed to provide attention, resources and investigative effort to the underlying criminal organization.

A comparison of both eras will help determine to what extent circumstances that allowed traditional organized crime to develop and flourish during Prohibition are present in the current drug era and what challenges must be faced in trying to overcome a development as nationally debilitating as is traditional organized crime.

ECONOMIC SCOPE--PROHIBITION

In economic terms Prohibition created an illegal market that affected the entire nation and reached beyond its borders. According to estimates, $90 million of illegal liquor was smuggled into the U.S. from 1922 to 1924. By 1923, 81 million gallons of denatured alcohol was produced for industry, an increase of 189 percent in six years without a comparable increase in industrial production. There were also estimates that the cash flow for organized crime rose to billions of dollars during the 1920s.

The illegal liquor industry in Detroit, as an example of one major city, provided 50,000 people with jobs in the smuggling, manufacture and distribution of alcohol. Its annual output was estimated at $215 million, placing it ahead of the chemical industry, and second only to automobile production in that city. Champagne, available in Canada for $4-7 a bottle, could be sold in Chicago, Detroit and New York for $20.

ECONOMIC SCOPE--DRUG ERA

According to a March 1987 report from the Office of Technology Assessment entitled the "Border War on Drugs," the size of the illegal economy supported by three drugs -- marijuana, cocaine and heroin -- was estimated to have an annual gross retail value in 1985 of about $50 billion, or equal to the combined sales of the nation's two largest retailers, Sears and K-Mart. More recent estimates (*U.S. News and World Report*, August 21, 1989) would double that figure to approximately $100 billion annually, or almost equal to General Motors' 1988 sales of $123 billion.

Consider the potential impact to the U.S. economy in terms of legitimate purchasing power if these billions of dollars involved were not diverted from the economy to illicit drug purchases. Perhaps the most dramatic figure defining the scope of the current drug market lies in the aforementioned *U.S. News and World Report* article, "Drug Money Laundering," in which the physical connection between money and drugs is described as so pervasive that random lab tests show virtually every U.S. bill in circulation (12 billion bills totalling $230 billion) bears microscopic traces of cocaine.

PRODUCT SOURCES--PROHIBITION

There were five major means of obtaining alcohol during Prohibition: smuggling (generally carried on from Canada, Mexico, the West Indies and the Bahamas); manufacturing (moonshine); illegal use of medical prescriptions; conversion of industrial alcohol to liquor; and strengthening the alcohol content of near beer.

PRODUCT SOURCES--DRUG ERA

The main source of the illicit U.S. drug market is smuggling through Asia, the Middle East, Mexico, Latin America and the Caribbean. Some manufacturing or processing of drugs takes place in the U.S., such as enhancement in crack houses, PCP and other synthetic drug labs, and, of course, there is also a major U.S. marijuana crop.

ORGANIZATIONAL/MANAGERIAL CHARACTERISTICS--PROHIBITION

Organized crime did not begin with Prohibition; Prohibition, however, provided the impetus for the sophistication of the organizations by their entry into the illegal liquor market. It required development of expertise in manufacturing, illegal importation, distribution, marketing and sales.

Ethnic-based organized crime groups re-invigorated the solidarity that had been diluted by the process of acculturation in American society. There were some common factors of the Prohibition gangs:

they were generally formed along ethnic lines to amass wealth and power; were territorially based; and were engaged in illegal and legal activities. A report on the Chicago protection rackets in December 1927 listed 23 separate lines of business exploited by racketeers and estimated that gangsters were actually in control of the destinies of over 90 necessary economic activities, such as dental laboratories and trash hauling. They operated with relatively low risk through insulation and had little regard for competition--their goal was to monopolize.

The gangs were also willing to use violence and corruption to achieve their goals. Between 1926 and 1930, for instance, 442 gangsters were killed in Chicago during rival gang feuding. The gangs maintained strong discipline and controlled memberships. Alliances were temporarily formed to establish territories and to promote individual organizational goals, and not least of all, to avoid disruption of profit flow by the diversion of resources ordinarily siphoned off during gang conflict.

The estimated cash flow in the '20s rose to billions of dollars and was the seed money for organized crime to move into other capital-intense criminal businesses such as loansharking and casino gambling, as well as to further expand into legitimate business. They had the organization, the warehouses, the know-how and the contracts which led to the development of national and international economic ties.

During the Prohibition era organized crime groups developed private sector and government relationships for economic and corruptive purposes. Organized crime became the prime source of political funds and other nefarious campaign support.

As their operations became more sophisticated, they became skilled at basic managerial tactics, having to ensure job assignments, security and enforcement of discipline. They also made use of staff and consulting services such as accountants, lawyers and investment consultants.

How good were they at providing the supply to meet the demand? The retail outlet of the Prohibition era was the speakeasy. According to testimony before the subcommittee of the Senate Judiciary Committee in April 1926, a witness estimated that throughout America there were three speakeasies for every old saloon.

ORGANIZATIONAL/MANAGERIAL CHARACTERISTICS--DRUG ERA

Focusing only on that segment of Prohibition prior to the monopolistic emergence of the traditional organized crime groups, one sees a striking similarity with the present status of ethnic and area-based drug trafficking groups.

The emergence of the ghetto gangs into drug trafficking on a major scale and the spread of their activities internationally is not unlike what occurred during Prohibition.

There is little question that some of the more aggressive urban gangs have begun to expand their drug activities into the heartland of America. An August 1989 report from federal attorneys across the nation to President Bush reports that illegal drug trafficking has spread from major cities, spawning new crime groups of contemporary Al Capones in rural areas, stretching across the country. This report identifies 43 principal drug trafficking organizations, including the Colombian cocaine cartels, La Cosa Nostra Family members and new Asian and Jamaican groups, that can be added to the list of participants in the drug market. The latter such group included street gangs, motorcycle gangs and regional crime organizations such as the "Dixie Mafia," Mexican Mafia and Cuban organized crime groups.

Like Prohibition era gangs, the drug era gangs also engage in legitimate as well as illegitimate businesses. One of the prime reasons for doing so is to aid in money laundering operations. One multicontinental scheme laundered $1 billion in three years through a floodgate of foreign banks, jewelry business fronts, gold brokers and wire transfers.

Like Prohibition era gangs, alliances are formed to increase profits mutually and avoid gang warfare, but the tremendous amount of violence associated with the drug era gangs also points to the lack of success in forming lasting alliances.

SOCIOLOGICAL/CULTURAL COMPARISONS--PROHIBITION

The enactment of Prohibition in 1920 was the result of years of debate and political wrangling by interest groups on both sides of the issue. It was by no means a result of unanimity among Americans. The argument for Prohibition was that it would be wholly beneficial. Drinking and intoxication would be reduced resulting in less absenteeism, a sober work force and greater productivity. As a moral issue families would not suffer as a result of the evils of alcohol which siphoned off hard-earned family funds from the necessities of life.

Perhaps the most persuasive indictment of Prohibition is that it led to a breakdown of law and order with the complicity of those in authority, and in fact, the remedy was worse than the disease.

The illicit market created by Prohibition became a great corrupting influence at all levels of society. There was an undermining of the basic foundation upon which this nation was built. In the first 11 years of the Prohibition Unit, the federal agency charged with Prohibition enforcement, there were 17,972 appointments, but there were also 11,982 resignations and 1,608 dismissals for corrupt practices.

A Prohibition bootlegger confided that he could not exist without the cooperation from the local and state police and 85 percent of the citizens. He related that "if you tell the average person you've got a load of liquor in your car, he'll hide you, lie for you, and help you." He described the help as being not only a physical help, but a moral help. It was reported that Al Capone paid bribes of approximately $30 million per year and his records listed half the area police force (*Prohibition*, Cashman, 1981).

Organized crime bosses were respected in lower-middle-class neighborhoods. They were looked upon as Robin Hoods who took from the rich and gave to the poor. Some had gregarious personalities and a working class sentimentality in their sense of morality. Consider the present situation in which the ghetto youth show adulation for the ostentatious lifestyles of drug peddlers.

SOCIOLOGICAL/CULTURAL CHARACTERISTICS--DRUG ERA

In 1988, approximately 28 million people used an illegal drug and 14.5 million, or approximately one in twenty, used an illegal drug during the month prior to the survey (National Household Survey On Drug Abuse).

There is a strong link between drug use and crime. In one period in New York City, 92 percent of those arrested for robbery and 80 percent of burglars tested positive for illegal drugs (White House Conference For A Drug Free America, Final Report, June 1988). Drug-related homicides are increasing drastically around the nation. Drug arrests, prosecutions and incarcerations are swamping the criminal justice system.

There is a drain of billions of dollars from the national economy. The impact on professions and the intelligentsia in terms of the loss of productivity and expertise, and the mental and physical effects of illicit use on children and future generations, is incalculable.

Like Prohibition, the illegal drug market has become a great corrupting influence. Law enforcement at the domestic level and on an international basis is being corrupted. Examples include reports of a drug ring operated by the Mexican Internal Security Force (*Time*,

March 7, 1988) and the reports that a substantial segment of the Miami City Police Force was implicated in a scheme to steal cocaine, sell it for profit and terrorize competition.

LAW ENFORCEMENT STRATEGIES--PROHIBITION

The enforcement strategies of Prohibition were investigation, seizure, destruction and interdiction. Investigation was primarily conducted by a federal agency, the Prohibition Bureau, that was generally underpaid, riddled with corruption and under-budgeted. Their enforcement tools were the "raid" and the "drive" which pooled law enforcement resources from the federal and state levels to cooperate in critical areas.

The Prohibition Bureau reported seizing 27,336 stills in 1929. In the fiscal year 1931, the value of bootlegging property seized was $21,484,730, and $3,447,558 in fines were collected. During the same period, 63,177 bootleggers were arrested by federal officers and 13,234 by state officers. An estimate of the total number of people involved in the liquor industry was well over 300,000.

Other strategies used to combat the illegal liquor market included increasing penalties for violations of the law. This strategy was a failure considering that even though the penalties were increased to felonies with fines of up to $10,000 or imprisonment of up to 5 years or both for the first offense, the national average of fines remained $130 and the average prison sentence 140 days. There were also diplomatic attempts in the way of search and seizure agreements regarding ships of several foreign countries.

LAW ENFORCEMENT STRATEGIES--DRUG ERA

One can only get a sense of deja vu from comparing enforcement strategies of the Prohibition and drug eras.

In 1987, at the federal level a total of $4 billion was divided among programs in the following percentages: 36 for interdiction, 10 for treatment, 7 for prevention, 6 for diplomatic initiatives, 2 for intelligence and 39 for enforcement.

The primary strategy for enforcement of the drug laws is interdiction and investigation. Enforcement efforts also include the tactics of interagency cooperation and the concentration on specific areas with joint operations through MEG (Metropolitan Enforcement Groups) and DEA (Drug Enforcement Administration). Penalties have been increased, including expanded laws to cover money-laundering operations; and asset forfeiture strategies have been developed as a tool to aid law enforcement.

There is basically a dual strategy in federal efforts to control drugs: reducing the supply of illicit drugs through enforcement and reducing the demand for drugs through prevention and treatment. These strategies are both national and international in scope. In the area of supply reduction, major initiatives include expanding the role of the military and U.S. intelligence community in drug enforcement.

In conclusion, it should be noted that one of the major advantages of law enforcement today that law enforcement of seven decades ago did not enjoy is advanced technology. In the area of information technology, for example, an August 1987 report prepared for the customs service found that removing drugs through interdiction is significantly more cost beneficial than through investigation efforts. The report showed that in 1986, on a retail value basis of cocaine and marijuana, a dollar of interdiction money resulted in $7.05 worth of cocaine and marijuana seizures; while a dollar of anti-drug investigation money yielded only $3.37 worth of cocaine and marijuana. The same report also found a relationship between increases in federal spending and a resultant rise in cocaine prices followed by a fall in cocaine consumption. Certainly, these analyses will become important in determining future law enforcement strategy.

Law enforcement must take advantage of sophisticated information technology and must integrate into its strategic planning sessions the potential for the negative "indirect" consequence previously mentioned.

If the drug era provides a fertile environment for criminal organizational emergence, as did Prohibition, should law enforcement diminish its efforts in other areas? Should prevention and youth training programs be reduced? No, because that is the most constructive, though long-term, area of demand reduction and social sanity. Nor should interdiction, arrests at all levels of this illicit market and asset seizures of principals' property be reduced. Communities would not allow it.

Diplomacy, aid and agreements at an international level must continue, as must efforts of drug rehabilitation. Millions of Americans, many of whom became addicted before an age at which they are considered qualified to vote or to enter into a contract, must not be "written off."

The effort must continue, through more effective coordination, unity and strategies, to overcome this threat to the nation. Awareness of past experiences, of the potentiality of criminal organizational sophistication, is an important first step. The increasing inclination to coordinate enforcement efforts and the technological advantages now available, particularly in the field of information exchange, must be pursued. Those criminal organizations that are emerging as the most "fit" can thereby be appropriately identified. It is they who are developing the organizational sophistication, the efficiencies of violent control, the monopolistic advance of market share and the resources for growth in other criminal areas and legitimate enterprise.

This is not meant to suggest an exact replica of the Prohibition script: this is a changed environment with higher stakes, more violence and a different cast. It is not at all clear, as Professor Moran implies in the August issue of *Newsweek*, that the traditional organized crime group will likely emerge from such conflict as the probable dominating force. Recall the thinking of those who confidently predicted the "big three" auto makers would easily regain their lost share of the automobile market after the Japanese grabbed a significant share of the market by producing a superior product at a reasonable price.

There are other gangs, other ghetto dwellers seeking the fast way out. There are other ethnic and racial groups not reliant upon the tenets of an old world social structure; they will use traditional organized crime as a standard or benchmark to emulate and surpass, with little need or regard for its hierarchy. With inappropriate law enforcement attention to criminal organization considerations, regional or multi-state criminal empires may develop which will be difficult to overcome because of the natural propensity of organizations to strive for perpetuity.

It is critical to first know of, and then direct coordinated organizational enforcement efforts to, the criminal enterprises that give evidence of "rising above the others." Attention to this indirect drug era potential consequence by all of law enforcement will go a long way to ensure that when this conflict is resolved, the enemy will have been overcome and will have retreated in disarray.

MATT L. RODRIGUEZ

Matt L. Rodriguez, a native Chicagoan, has been a member of the Chicago Police Department since 1959. He has served through the ranks of the department, being promoted from Detective, to Sergeant, and to Lieutenant in 1978 as Commanding Officer of an Area Youth Division; Commanding Officer of the City-Wide Gambling Division; and Administrative Assistant to the superintendent; and Deputy Superintendent. His career background includes a myriad of assignments, with service in Patrol, Training, Detective, and Organized Crime Divisions of the Chicago Police Department.

Deputy Superintendent Rodriguez has a Master's Degree in Public Administration and is a 1977 graduate of Northwestern University Traffic

Institutes' Management Program. He has participated in the Harvard University/Police Executive Research Forum's comprehensive Management Training Program. He is also a member of the Adjunct Faculty of the Criminal Justice Department, the University of Illinois at Chicago.

Rodriguez is presently the Deputy Superintendent, Bureau of Technical Services, where he is responsible for administering seven of the Chicago Police Department's major divisions.

ORGANIZED CRIME POLICY IN THE UNITED KINGDOM

Simon Crawshaw

The English language is an extremely flexible and versatile means of communication and this is manifestly so in the use of the phrase "organized crime."

The English dictionary definition of the term "organize" is reasonably precise: "to provide with an organic structure, to make plans and arrange." The dictionary definition, however, would include the vast majority of criminal conspiracies which require a degree of premeditation.

Notwithstanding the policeman's interpretation of the term "organized crime," it is the interpretation of the term by the public, and many public officials, that causes the greatest obstacle when attempting to pursue those involved. In addition, the term can mean different things in different nations. A type of criminal activity falling within a definition in one jurisdiction may be excluded in another.

Those who seek the assistance of the law in defining crime are equally frustrated; certainly as far as the English law is concerned no such definition exists.

The question at this point is whether there is a need to precisely define the phenomenon. Probably not, and to do so would be restrictive and counter-productive.

From a police officer's point of view, the lack of a precise definition has its disadvantages. If you cannot define it, how can you ask for the government to legislate against it? How can you convince those who control the purse strings that dedicated resources have to be allocated to deal specifically with the problem?

Some police forces and even governments through their inability to recognize the symptoms have been unsuccessful in dealing with organized crime. Many senior police officers and government officials have, it would appear, sought to emulate the famous English seaman Lord Nelson who had been charged to engage, at first sight, the French fleet. However, for tactical reasons, on the approach of the French, he placed his telescope to his blind eye and declared "I see no ships." Similarly the statement "I have no organized crime" may at first appear as an attempt to equal the great seaman's tactical arrogance; however, such statements can often be born out of naivety, incompetence or, at worst, political gerrymandering.

If challenged, an individual who holds such views could easily retort, relying upon the public perception of organized crime, "We have no Don Corleone or Al Capone in this area." Usually the only counter to such a statement is "Perhaps not at present, but by the time you're able to identify such a figurehead it will be too late."

The criminal empire ruthlessly ruled by Al Capone, like an oak tree, had an acorn origin, which subsequently grew. It is well documented that in the 1920s and 1930s the insidious and debilitating effect of organized crime was not at first appreciated. The problem was allowed to develop to the point where the welfare and security of the affected states were threatened because of corrupt highly placed public officials. It was not until the full extent of this damage was realized that funds and resources were made available to pursue in earnest those involved. A significant degree of the damage inflicted, however, was irreparable and a large proportion of the profits generated by the various organized crime families had been laundered and was irretrievable. The Task Squad at New Scotland Yard, responsible for the investigation of organized crime in London, learned a number of lessons from the Capone investigation.

To return to the question posed earlier, which affects policy on organized crime in Britain: If police were to wait until all the ingredients of a precise definition of organized crime were present, then there could well be another Al Capone figure in place. It would be too late to prevent the corruption of public officials in the judiciary and in government - - the rot would have already set in. The resources and finances required to remove such a threat at that juncture would also be prohibitive. Even more extreme, as has happened in countries where corrupt officials were placed in key positions, the necessary government financial backing could be lacking or compromised.

In Britain the police service, through their various public relations offices, has gone to great lengths to educate the public and government that organized crime exists in the U.K. It is not a formally structured, hierarchical organization with one individual controlling and running his operation, but, rather, it is a loose-knit, intricate web of associations where individuals are selected for their particular skills.

The flexibility of the extended family concept allows major criminals to band together when necessary to commit serious crime. Features of a business enterprise are recognizable with specifically qualified individuals specializing on the operational side (acquisition, marketing and distribution), while others supply the support services (finance, accounting and legal) which also involves the laundering and disposal of assets.

Although the features highlighted previously are generally accepted, Scotland Yard has also learned from past mistakes. For many years, there has been successful investigation of serious crime and prosecution of major criminals. Until recently, however, the tendency has been to concentrate on individual cases or individual criminals. Prominent criminals have been given custodial sentences, often of salutary length. However, more often than not, in their absence, their relatives and lieutenants have been able to manage and develop their ill-gotten gains, thereby providing a cushion against the inconvenience of the prison sentence and an invested financial operating base, in the event of early or eventual release. Such prosecutions have little effect on the organizers of major crime and its beneficiaries. In effect police were lopping off the branches of major crime without seriously damaging the roots of the proverbial oak tree.

In the demise of Al Capone there were lessons learned, bearing in mind the mobster's incarceration was for revenue offenses only. It is now a recognized part of our investigative policy that to disrupt organized crime activities, an attack must be made on its other works: the proceeds.

With the prolific increase in Britain of drug crime (and to a lesser extent fraud) where the proceeds and profits are enormous, it became evident that to make any impression on the increasing numbers of those thus employed, additional legislation would be needed. Such legislation would enable police to trace and follow the complex web of money laundering ventures that were operating with a view to sequestration.

In drug trafficking, Britain can now rely upon the Drug Trafficking Offenses Act 1986, which gives police new powers to obtain access to information about a person's financial affairs at an early stage of a drug trafficking investigation. Once a conviction has been received, the Act provides that the court *must* make a confiscation order if it appears that a person has profited from drug crimes. In April 1989, the Criminal Justice Act provided similar powers with regards to other serious crime. The main difference between the two items of legislation is that in the former Act the court has no discretion and *must* make an order of confiscation. However, in the Criminal Justice Act, this provision is discretionary.

Certainly as far as drug trafficking and fraud were concerned, and major armed robberies to a lesser extent, the view had long been expressed that the main organizer of such crimes stayed close to the financial gains and as far from acts of crime as possible. In addition to using illegally obtained funds for expansion and survival within the criminal sphere, organized crime is primarily concerned with legitimizing its money as a means to ultimate long-term protection. The majority of criminals of the calibre being discussed earnestly seek legitimacy. If they cannot achieve such a goal within their own lifespan, they desire it for their offspring. To achieve this aim, profits must be laundered to obscure their illicit origin. As a result, organized crime has, by necessity, perfected techniques to collate monies from criminal ventures, processing and refining that wealth so as to hide its true origin.

The processes involved are legion and invariably include the movement of money or some other valuable commodity through different national jurisdictions and often through so-called offshore financial centers.

The greater the degree of secrecy obtained during this process the better. Consequently, those jurisdictions which, for often acceptable business reasons, offer bank secrecy and commercial confidentiality are obviously attractive conduits.

In order to pursue the financial assets as a strategic aim, there is a need also, through the Financial Branch, for government to provide sufficient funds to carry out the task.

To understand the policy of major crime investigation in London and other parts of the United Kingdom, it is necessary to appreciate that, as with other public sector services in Britain, there is a restricted budget. When obliged to run an organization on finite resources, difficult and often unpopular decisions must be made. This is especially so regarding which major crime operations can be afforded and which, through lack of resources, must be placed in the pending tray.

Specialist Operations at New Scotland Yard is part of the largest police force in the United Kingdom; to an extent it has been able to apportion its budget into crime investigative initiatives with a minimum of interference from the government. The Metropolitan Police, to which Specialist Operations at New Scotland Yard belongs, is one of 52 police forces in the United Kingdom, each with its own budget. Only the very large forces (about six) are able, with present budgeting arrangements, to sustain any major prolonged initiative against organized crime in their particular force area.

In addition, all police forces within the United Kingdom are obliged to manage their budgets on the monetary principle of VFM - - Value For Money. In order to justify an expenditure or seek an increase in a budget, it is necessary to quantify, in precise terms, the benefits derived from such expenditure. At best, inquiries into organized crime can take months before a result is achieved. In serious cases investigations can run into years.

As indicated previously, organized crime is imprecise and in its early stages, to the uninitiated, there is no perception of any problem. It is therefore extremely difficult to justify the apportionment of funds in such cases. This problem is compounded by the need for absolute secrecy during the preparatory intelligence gathering process which must necessarily precede such an investigation. The difficulty in financing organized crime investigations in certain parts of the country has, regretfully, become very acute.

Because of the alarming expansion in international drug crime and the increasing propensity of indigenous criminals to travel abroad and serve as liaisons to foreign criminal groups, there is increasing support for the need for a single force in the United Kingdom to deal with such individuals. It is envisaged that such a force would be organized and financed on a similar basis to that of the DEA or FBI in the United States.

New Scotland Yard has been fortunate in the past; however, it is important to remember that, generally speaking, it is responsible for the policing of London only. Having said "only", be assured that it is more than enough responsibility.

In keeping with recognized budgeting principles and sound police investigative policy, Task Squad operations are selected by a means of prioritization. From available intelligence sources, a number of groups will be targeted. Targeting in the first instance will entail obtaining additional intelligence and confirming other information already possessed or given by a registered informant. Usually a period of time is set for the Criminal Intelligence Branch to complete this task. A conference is then held among the Branch Commanders and on the basis of the perceived threat, the list is reduced until two or three groups remain.

These remaining groups are then subjected to increased surveillance. New Scotland Yard refers to this particular intelligence gathering procedure as Collection Plans. During this process individuals will not be arrested, unless absolutely necessary, until the comprehensive intelligence gathering process is finished.

When this process has been completed, the Specialist Intelligence Section of the Criminal Intelligence Branch will give a presentation to the Deputy Assistant Commissioner and the Branch Commanders. They will then select the group considered to pose the greatest threat and adopt that group as the Task Squad target, devoting all available resources to terminate their enterprises.

The other groups which were not selected are either held in reserve or passed to other Specialist Operations Squads. After the selection of the target group, the Specialist Operations Task Squad continues to rely upon the Specialist Intelligence Section for the development of available intelligence. In addition the specialist officers employed within the squad who have been drawn from fraud, drugs and other serious crime branches, channel all new intelligence through the same section.

On the subject of intelligence, the Metropolitan Police have an integrated intelligence system which culminates in a pool system available to all investigators. Simply, all the various investigative branches have their own computerized intelligence data bases; however, all these data bases can be searched from a central pool within the Criminal Intelligence Branch. The theory behind the pool system is that which once took 20 telephone calls can now be achieved efficiently with one. Obviously for security reasons, active and confidential intelligence will be held at a secure level; however, to avoid duplication of effort, human checks have been built into the system.

The Task Squad at New Scotland Yard was established in 1985. The squad's ability to combat organized crime through its financial base was almost immediately exercised when information was received regarding disposal of assets following the Brink's-Mat robbery at Heathrow Airport in 1983 when gold bullion valued at $39 million was stolen.

Inquiries under the auspices of Operation Cougar targeted a British solicitor, Patrick Diamond, who ran a number of companies from his commercial base on the Isle of Man. From intelligence sources Diamond was known to associate with prominent American and British crime figures.

Following the seizure of documents from Diamond's offices and diligent inquiries by the Task Squad detectives, a line of bank accounts and companies was discovered. It soon became apparent that the Brink's-Mat money was only a small part of a large illicit fund which included a significant amount of American drug money. This money was traced traveling through the various accounts, much of which was being laundered by British banks in colonies in the Caribbean Islands.

As a result of this discovery, close cooperation was established between the task squad, the Drug Enforcement Agency and other U.S. federal authorities in Miami who set in motion a similar inquiry code-named "Operation MAN."

Cooperation on this specific inquiry continued for two years during which time 25 major U.S. drug dealers were indicted before American courts, and more than $100 million worth of proceeds were seized. In addition, following inquiries in Liechtenstein, Switzerland and Ireland, a large quantity of the proceeds of the Brink's-Mat robbery was located and seized and a number of British citizens, including a well-known attorney, have been dealt with by the courts for their part in disposing of the assets.

While it is difficult to obtain agreement on what constitutes organized crime, it is universally accepted that the phenomenon, as a result of worldwide drug abuse, continues to grow and cannot be restricted by local or international borders. Operation COUGAR/MAN demonstrated to the British government in unequivocal terms that if police are to have any success in the future in this area of law enforcement, they will have to dispense with their current parochial municipal policing mentality.

SIMON CRAWSHAW

Mr. Crawshaw was born in Porth, Cornwall, and educated at Haileybury and Imperial Services College, Hertford, and at The Norfolk School of Agriculture.

He joined the Metropolitan Police on June 4, 1962, and served as a Police Constable and Detective Constable at a number of stations in South London. Several promotions followed during which time he attended a Special Course at the Police Staff College, Bramshill and, as Detective Inspector in A8 Branch at New Scotland Yard, was involved in the operation of the Police helicopter unit. He has attended the Intermediate and Senior Command Courses at the Police Staff College at Bramshill. Mr. Crawshaw was subsequently appointed Operational Head of the Central Robbery Squad, responsible for the prevention, investigation and detection of major robberies, including all armed robberies, in the Metropolitan Police area.

In January 1983, Mr. Crawshaw was appointed Commander 2 Area with overall responsibility for the investigation of crime in North West and Central London. On November 5, 1984, Mr. Crawshaw was appointed head of the Anti-Terrorist Branch and on August 6, 1985, he was promoted to Deputy Assistant Commissioner and assumed responsibility for Special Branch and the Anti-Terrorist Branch. On December 1, 1987, Mr. Crawshaw was appointed Deputy Assistant Commissioner, Specialist Operations, responsible for the International Organized Crime Branch, the Serious Crime Branch, the Fraud Branch and the Criminal Intelligence Branch.

Mr. Crawshaw was awarded the Queen's Police Medal in June 1987.

THE ROLE OF THE COURTS IN COMBATING INTERNATIONAL CRIME

Aldo Grassi

INTRODUCTION AND THE GENERAL CONCEPT OF THE JUDICIARY

In order to explain the role of the Courts of Justice in the battle against international crime, it is essential to agree on the concept of the judiciary, its purpose and the role of magistrates.

The oldest and most common concept of the judicial function is as one of the three essential functions of the State, defined in relation to the legislative and executive functions. This definition proceeds from intuitive knowledge of the difference between the various functions of the State and attempts to formulate the essence of the judicial function. From this point of view, the judicial function encompasses the realization of rights, the settlement of lawsuits, the enforcement of sanctions and the substitution of public actions for private ones. It is an approach that contains elements of truth, because all the factors can be included in the judicial function even if they do not exhaust the concept.

A misunderstanding lies at the basis of similar attempts to define the judiciary: the premise that it is only a function of the State. Indeed, the reference to the State on the subject of the judiciary only makes sense when talking about power, as judicial authority implies the concept of power, but its purposes are, certainly, far deeper and broader.

The reference to the State is made, first of all, from a historical point of view and assigns judicial authority exclusively to the State, as a product of its sovereignty. But when we talk about the judiciary as being one of the three functions of the State, in reality our aim is that of expressing a political principle, according to which society is organized into the three fundamental branches--legislative, executive and judicial--by applying abstract principles to real cases.

Consideration must be given, however, to the fact that the social community is organized in a more complex way and that the concept of the judiciary finds its most fundamental role in the application of the legal system and its rules to all the complex events of daily life.

All this leads to an important consideration: without the judiciary a State's legal system would fail, since a system is juridical only insofar as it is authoritatively maintained.

Legislation precedes the judicial function, and the latter guarantees the compliance and the legality of the former. The definition of the judiciary as the application of the legal system in actual cases contains the implicit indication of the way in which jurisdiction itself is fulfilled.

On this subject the emphasis falls on "actual cases" which, when analyzed, may be divided into the following:

a) subjective cases, in which the system can be affirmed only as regards one individual;

b) objective cases, because the necessity of applying the system assumes that something actually appears not to conform to it; and

c) cases relevant to both subjective and objective interests towards the re-affirmation of the violated law system to guarantee a stable and orderly society.

The reenforcement of the legal system which has been violated by the illegal behavior of some citizens takes place according to the rules of the court case.

The conceptual unity of the judiciary does not exclude the fact that distinctions must be made. The diversity of each case deeply reflects on the way the judicial function is carried out and brings to light different interests which affect the various forms and types of trial.

As regards criminal proceedings, which are carried out through penal action, it must be observed that criminal law--by tracing the border line between lawful and unlawful--constitutes the utmost expression of state organization.

In the criminal trial, two separate interests emerge: that of the community in upholding the law and in re-establishing the social balance, and that of the defendant in having his own personal freedom respected.

It is easy to understand that the problems involved in the judicial function belong to the highest sphere of judicial speculation, a fact which justifies research on a theoretical level. Nevertheless, research on a practical level is also necessary and this paper is restricted to the criminal field.

CRIMINAL JURISDICTION IN GENERAL

On the subject of criminal law one can talk about the judiciary having both a static and a dynamic profile.

The former has two aspects: one is abstract, and refers to the State's power to have laws enforced as an expression of its sovereignty; the other is concrete, and refers to the bodies through which the State exercises judicial authority in separate cases. The dynamic profile also has two aspects, in which "criminal" is seen as both the activity set up by the bodies endowed with the power to apply criminal law to citizens, and the legitimatizing of such bodies to exercise the power conferred to them.

Magistrates, to whom the exercise of criminal judicial authority is reserved, must first of all be impartial. They must place themselves as *super partes* and leave determination of the defendant's guilt until the final moment of the trial, when judgement is pronounced.

The task of ascertaining by means of the trial whether an accusation is grounded in fact is strictly reserved for judges of criminal law. This means that they have the task of establishing whether a specific action is considered by law as an offense, and also whether it was the accused who consciously and willfully committed it.

Only if these two factors can be attributed to the defendant, and the act is an offense at law, must the judge come to a decision on the guilt of the individual and inflict a penalty on the defendant.

But at this point the following questions should be posed: Why punish? How to punish? Who to punish? Before answering questions such as these, it is necessary to be aware of the considerable qualitative and quantitative increases over the past 20 years in common and organized crime, both on a national and international scale.

We are dealing with crime levels which, on one hand, threaten individuals' lives and liberties and, on the other, undermine public life. Theft, armed robberies, extortion, kidnapping and murders are, unfortunately, now day-to-day occurrences. Well-trained criminal organizations seriously affect the lives of entire regions.

The consequent growing social alarm manifests itself as an ever-growing demand for safety from the State. The State, then, looks to its constitutional powers for a more efficient deterrent solution. Such a solution, though, seems inadequate if unaccompanied by suitable measures to remove the causes of criminality.

It is for this reason that, at both a legislative and a judicial level, there has been a general increase of penal repression in many countries, coincident with lowered public demand for security.

Therefore, the increased interest shown towards the problem of reducing crime is understandable, and many scholars are dedicating their attention to it. In light of the most recent experiences it is easy to understand why there is a return to the study of the function of punishment, of its ethical and political meaning, of its philosophical justification and of its aims and limits.

This serves as introduction to an old investigation, proposed in a new light, and dictated by today's experiences. Besides being rich in practical implications, this approach appears to be appropriate theoretically since sanctions, of which punishment is the most typical expression, constitute the essential element of the lawfulness of legal rules.

There are many theories on the nature and purposes of punishment. An early theory is that punishment should be carried out because a crime has been committed; another theory is that the purpose of punishment is to prevent other crimes. This distinction, adopted by Anglo-Saxon scholars, basically corresponds to the German and Italian doctrines. In the absolutist approach, punishment justifies itself, while the relativist approach views punishment as only the means to an end. The former sees punishment only as a penalty; the latter sees it as an instrument of prevention and correction.

The most intransigent theory of punishment as penalty or moral retribution goes back to the German philosopher Immanuel Kant. According to this theory a criminal is punished simply because he has committed a crime, and the punishment is justified solely by a compulsory need for justice.

The Kantian concept of criminal law presages that of another philosopher, Hegel, who saw punishment as a strictly judicial, and not moral, retribution that ensures that through the infliction of punishment the law is re-affirmed.

Theories of punishment as moral or judicial retribution have been largely disfavored, first, because they seem to be irrational and limiting; and second, because it is an unacceptable expression of revenge to think of inflicting punishment as an end to itself.

Yet, these theories have the merit of having set principles by which the guilty individual can be punished, while maintaining a proper balance between the severity of the punishment and the gravity of the crime.

The doctrine of prevention or defense headed by the Italian Domenico Romagnosi and the German Anselm Feuerbach belongs to the group of relativist theories, which do not consider punishment as an end in itself.

According to these theories, society has a right to defend itself from those who, by violating the law, endanger an orderly society. Such a defense can be carried out by the infliction of punishment, the fear of which has a deterrent effect on potential wrong-doers.

Basically, punishment helps to establish the principle whereby crime does not pay, and therefore it becomes "inconvenient" to violate the law.

Within this theory a distinction must be made between special and general prevention, according to whether the intimidating force of punishment is directed only at the guilty individual or at other citizens as well. In other words, punishment must help to dissuade whoever has committed a crime from committing other crimes and to dissuade others from manifesting anti-social behavior similar to that which caused the infliction of penal punishment.

The most frequent criticism of the theory of punishment as a means of prevention is that it may bring about a sort of "penal terrorism." Excessively severe punishment may be disproportionate to the crime committed.

Some scholars consider punishment as an instrument of re-education of the offender and as a means of his or her rehabilitation. This theory, known as the theory of amendment, exalts the corrective nature of punishment, and assigns it the noble aim of improving whoever has erred; it sees punishment, therefore, not as an evil but as something beneficial to the individual concerned.

This theory has also been criticized because it assigns to the State the power of evaluating the moral behavior of its citizens, a power that the State should not have, and which would foster a paternalistic attitude of dubious legitimacy.

Another criticism of the theory of amendment is that it impairs the fundamental principle of the "certainty of rights." Since it is not possible to establish in advance at which point the criminal will be fully rehabilitated, the punitory action may continue indefinitely.

In response to these differing doctrines of punishment, a theory has developed that regards punishment as a means of social defense. This theory encompasses both the principles of amendment and of prevention, but emphasizes the social character of the latter.

According to this theory, punishment must be of use in defending society from the perpetration of crimes, and therefore cannot only be a penalty. It must be accompanied by other measures, for example, educational intervention, economic assistance and health therapy.

In this way, the concepts of guilt and responsibility give way to those of "social danger," by which the offender is no longer considered only a guilty person to be punished, but a sick person to be cured.

Obviously, each of these theories has positive aspects, but not one of them alone provides a satisfactory answer to the numerous difficulties posed by the so-called "criminal question."

This latter can be summed up in the necessity to face the phenomenon of delinquency in a way which will suitably guarantee, on the one hand, the social order threatened by crime, and on the other, the freedom and dignity of man, which are to be safeguarded even vis-a-vis a guilty individual.

The functions of the traditional goals of prevention, retribution and amendment, in the three stages of the punitory process--determination, infliction and the carrying out of the punishment--bring to mind the idea that prevention, retribution and amendment are not three different answers to the same question, but, on the contrary, are three different answers to three different questions; that is, "Why punish?", "Who to punish?" and "How to punish?."

The first of these three questions is directed at the legislator, who has the responsibility of the defense of social order. The doctrine of prevention and social defense supplies an adequate reply to this question. In fact, the aim of criminal law is the defense of judicial order through the prevention of criminal behavior by means of intimidatory force deriving from the threat of punishment against law transgressors.

The question "Who to punish?", is directed, above all, at the magistrate, to whom falls the task of inflicting the punishment on a specific individual. The norms, issued by the legislature, are general and abstract, while the magistrate's decision is individual and concrete; it has a clearly identified object - the offender.

To the question "Who to punish?," the theory of retribution provides a suitable reply, in that the judgment of guilt can be formulated and the punishment inflicted only on the individual whose criminal act has the material and psychological causal relations. Furthermore, the principle of retribution provides a reasonable balance between the severity of punishment and the gravity of the crime, thus avoiding the transformation of punishment into revenge.

And finally, the theory of amendment answers the question "How to punish?." In the execution phase, punishment must aim at the re-education of the offender and at his or her subsequent social rehabilitation. Another objective must be that of demonstrating that if the threat of punishment does not deter the commission of a crime, it nevertheless must be inflicted in order to restore the disturbed social order. In the long term, the threat of punishment will help to deter other potential offenders.

Some important considerations arise from the amendment theory of punishment: the opposition to inhumane punishment and the rejection of the death penalty (which precludes any possibility of rehabilitation).

Precisely because punishment deeply affects fundamental principles such as liberty and honor, it must be respectful of those values.

With this in mind, it is the legislator's task to use punishment cautiously in order to avoid the monopoly of the use of force which the State claims for itself.

It is the magistrate's duty to suit the punishment to the gravity of the crime, after having rigorously ascertained the guilt of the defendant. This must obviously be carried out with scrupulous observance of the trial regulations, and without the influence of the mass media and pubic pressure.

INTERNATIONAL CRIME

The problem of international crime must be considered in light of a realistic vision of the power of international law as a system of organization of social life.

According to an idea largely adopted by jurists, international law is a universal legal system, with the task of regulating human conduct in respect to which the legal systems of separate States are seen as derived from it.

The fact that individuals are subject to the authority of the State to which they belong means that international law is generally directed toward countries and not individual citizens. Likewise, individuals are considered, within international law, as representing national governments, whose activities are authorized or prohibited by international law.

Consequently, international law considers individuals as the center of interest worthy of international protection, as well as centers of human activities that can satisfy or impair internationally protected interests.

The duty of international law, therefore, is to set down norms for individual nations in order that they may govern their peoples so that just interests are safeguarded and prejudicial actions against internationally protected interests are discouraged, while those activities from which similar interests may take advantage are favored.

International regulations require the State to punish citizens for committing crimes of an international nature over which they have jurisdiction.

It is a difficult task to determine principles by which human activities are protected by international law or are to be considered as international crimes.

The most common definition, and an inadequate one, is that only those activities which are identified and subjected to international law may be viewed as international crimes. This theory, supported by the Commission for International Law of the United Nations Assembly, assumes that the international legal system can directly impose sanctions on individuals, regardless of the national laws of the single States.

It must be observed that the international community cannot yet rely on bodies through which it might assert its authority directly on individuals. Currently, only States can exert their authority on citizens and take punitive measures for international crimes.

An international crime occurs when it infringes on the interests of all humanity, or when the international community considers itself to be directly damaged.

In truth, the borderline between international and other crimes, which a State is obliged to recognize in order to meet the demands of international order, cannot always be traced clearly and with absolute certainty. This uncertainty cannot be overcome until the definition of international crime is clearly understood by the international community, and not until bodies of the international community have the power to intervene to punish them.

A traditional category of international crimes is that of "war crimes," which consist of serious violations of "war laws" identified and listed in precise international conventions (for example, the Geneva Convention, 12th August, 1949, Art. I30; the Washington Treaty, 16th February, 1922, art.3).

The "Code about Crimes Against the Peace and Safety of Mankind," elaborated by the Commission for International Law in its 1954 edition, defines war crimes as "acts in violation of the laws or customs of war." Moreover, according to terminology used in the Hague Convention in 1899 and 1907, the basic reference for laws and customs of war is meant to be the international normative law relevant to the war conduct.

In addition to "war crimes," piracy--acts performed by crews or sea-going people, not on behalf of a State, that offend the liberty of the high seas and the safety of navigation--is generally considered to be an international crime. Pirates are subject to the authority of any State that apprehends them.

International crimes also include those offenses against peace and mankind, the identification of which came about after the Second World War.

The Nuremberg Court maintained that the "winning powers" of the Second World War were permitted, by international law, to punish subjects or bodies of the defeated countries for having committed crimes against peace and humanity.

War crimes, as well as those against peace and mankind, are viewed as international crimes and demand cooperation among countries. There is a need for the codification and development of general principles of international law and the adoption of procedural regulations. The necessity of arranging adequate bodies to administer justice is also important.

THE INTERNATIONAL JUDICIARY

In the international legal system, both the jurisdiction and the constitution of the judging body exist on an exclusively voluntary basis; that is, they exist only where there is jurisdiction for specific cases. This may be "general," if set up for eventual or future controversies, or "special," if referring to a real controversy that has already occurred.

General jurisdiction provides permanent courts that permit single States to apply when a violation occurs.

Among the most important of these are the European Court of Justice, and the European Court for Human Rights.

The jurisdiction of the International Court of Justice is granted by Art. 30 of its Statute and Regulations, and in various agreements set up by countries interested in settling controversies in the Court.

The International Court of Justice can be appealed to, not by individuals or other international organizations, but by the countries which, on the basis of Art. 93 of the United Nations Treaty, are members of this organization and by those non-member countries that are willing to adhere to the Statute and accept the conditions set by the United Nations General Assembly.

According to Art. 36 of the Statute, the authority of the International Court is extended to all issues that the parties deem advisable to submit to it and, furthermore, to those cases arising under a United Nations Treaty, or by other treaties or conventions in force.

The agreement whereby a given controversy is submitted to the decision of an International Court, is called "compromise." This attributes to the Court jurisdiction over the controversy.

International Courts, appointed to deal with controversies between countries, do not have any authority to judge international crimes carried out by private individuals or non-state organizations.

INTERNATIONAL CONNECTIONS AND ORGANIZED CRIME

Increasing organized crime makes it necessary to recognize that criminal organizations with links to other countries also operate within single countries. International drug and weapon trafficking, as well as the exploitation of women for prostitution, are current examples of such crimes.

It is well-known that many narcotic substances are produced in some States, transported to others where they are refined and then distributed in other countries by means of a network of well-connected criminal organizations.

In the same way it is well known that many criminal associations commit offenses using weapons secretly imported from other countries, and individuals cross the borders of a State--often illegally and under a false name--to carry out crimes and acts of political terrorism.

Large criminal organizations are also involved in criminal trafficking in prostitution and drugs.

The general rule gives judicial authority to each country to judge and punish whomever has committed a crime on its national territory including non-citizens.

Where other countries may be involved, co-operation, in some cases already provided for and sanctioned by international conventions, is absolutely necessary and constitutes the premise used to identify and prosecute criminal organizations that act on an international level.

I believe that cooperation must not be entrusted - as it has been on some occasions - to the intelligent and appreciable initiative of single magistrates or the Prosecuting Attorney's Office, but must be provided for and regulated by adequate national law and precise international conventions.

To face up to international crime, countries should organize themselves in both legislative and operative ways if they want to avoid the risk of being unable to stand up to the phenomenon of organized crime. To this end cooperation should exist, above all, between the police and the Prosecuting Attorney's Offices.

It is vital to create a situation whereby the exchange of information in data banks at the disposal of police bodies, judicial departments and the courts of individual countries is permanent.

At the same time, it is necessary to broaden the clauses extradition treaties to help recover those who find refuge in other countries.

It also seems necessary that judges be professionally trained to understand and evaluate certain criminal phenomena in their real international dimension.

To consider certain phenomena such as political terrorism, or organized crime in a narrow-minded and short-sighted way as issues only of national importance, is a big mistake, and will assure defeat in the battle against crime.

In the fight against international crime it is essential to have well-trained Magistrates who are equipped with the means and instruments that will allow them to understand criminal phenomena that cross national borders. Only in this way can the penalties inflicted by these Magistrates be considered suitable and adequate punishment for the guilty individual.

Punishment can then be seen as an attempt to rehabilitate offenders and carry out the essential functions of general and special prevention, which protects the dignity and the freedom of man.

ALDO GRASSI

Dr. Aldo Grassi was awarded the degree of Jurisprudence in 1961, where he graduated with honors from the University of Catania in Sicily. He was then asked to accept the position of Assistant Professor and Academic Chair of Constitutional Law at the Faculty of Jurisprudence at that same university. Two years after his graduation he passed an open competition and obtained a post of Magistrate where he has exercised his role as both Civil and Penal Judge, and Solicitor General in various parts of Sicily.

Since 1985, Dr. Grassi has been a member of the Bench of the 1st Penal Section of the Law Courts of Messina and was also a member of the Judging Bench for a Maxi-Trial which dealt with 285 defendants accused of association with known delinquents and criminals at a Mafia level.

He is a Founder Member of the Council of Administration and of the Scientific Committee of the International Centre of Sociological, Penal and penitentiary Research and Studies of Messina.

On merit alone, Dr. Grassi was recently appointed to the Supreme Court of Cassation in Rome, Italy, as Legal Advisor for the 1st Penal Section of Italy. The Supreme Court of Cassation is the highest body of the Italian Jurisdiction, whose task is to assure a precise application of the law by the judges during penal procedures.

ASSET FORFEITURE: Civil Remedies Against Organized Crime

Robert M. Lombardo

This paper discusses the use of civil forfeiture as a tool against organized crime. Both the Organized Crime Control Act of 1970 and Federal Controlled Substances Act provide for the forfeiture of property used in violation of these statutes. This paper briefly reviews these laws and provides current examples of their application to organized crime enforcement.

There has long been a call for civil remedies in the fight against organized crime. The 1967 President's Task Force Report recommended the use of civil proceedings to stop unfair trade practices and antitrust violations by organized crime controlled businesses. These recommendations were codified in the Racketeer Influenced Corrupt Organizations Act (RICO) of 1970 which includes provisions for divesting a person of his interest in an illegal enterprise, the restraint of future activities and the dissolution or reorganization of such enterprises.

The Organized Crime Control Act of 1970 added forfeiture to the list of civil remedies directed against organized crime by making all property used to further an illegal gambling business forfeitable to the United States. Forfeiture is a legal proceeding that enforces obedience to a law by transferring to the government property that has been used in violation of the law. Congress also amended the Controlled Substances Act in 1978 declaring that all assets acquired from the illicit drug trade belong to the United States government and are subject to civil seizure under the forfeiture power. This Act was strengthened in 1984 when Congress again changed the Controlled Substances Act to allow for the forfeiture of real property used to facilitate drug violations.

An important aspect of these laws is that property seized by local and state officers can be transferred to a federal agent who can in effect "adopt" the seizure just as though it had originally been seized by him. Authority to adopt seizures can be traced to the decisions of the Supreme Court (Dodge v. U.S., 47 S.Ct.191 [1926]) and to English common law which held that anyone had the right to seize outlaws and outlawed property (Hoffman, 1987). State and local officers may thus benefit from the power of these federal statutes when their state does not permit forfeiture or when state law is more restrictive than federal law. This paper will examine the forfeiture provisions of these laws, through a review of several recent Chicago Police Department cases, and demonstrate their potential as weapons against organized crime.

ORGANIZED CRIME CONTROL ACT

The Organized Crime Control Act of 1970 makes it a criminal offense to conduct, finance or manage an illegal gambling business. An "illegal gambling business" is one which is in violation of state law or a political subdivision thereof; involves five or more persons; and has been in substantially continuous operation for more than thirty days or has a gross revenue of more than $2,000 in any single day. Title 18 Section 1955 (d) of the United States Code states that "Any property, including money, used in violation of the provisions of this section may be seized and forfeited to the United States."

In spite of being the major source of revenue for traditional organized crime, many jurisdictions do not see gambling as a serious crime problem. Law enforcement officers know only too well that the investigation and prosecution of this so-called victimless crime often takes a back seat to crimes of violence and other serious offenses. But gambling is not a victimless crime. The revenue derived from gambling has been used by criminal syndicates to corrupt unions and government, finance narcotics and vice operations and generally destroy the moral fabric of many of the nation's urban areas. As such, society itself is the victim of this crime.

Those convicted of syndicated gambling and other serious gambling offenses at the local level usually receive no more than probation in criminal court. Even at the federal level, the most sophisticated gambling prosecutions usually result in short prison terms. Criminal sanctions, therefore, may provide little deterrent to illegal gambling. Thus gamblers, even more than narcotic dealers, are willing to risk arrest and prosecution because of the profits derived from this offense. Forfeiture law is designed to attack this motive by taking illegal profits from criminal organizations and diverting them to the very society that they have harmed.

A classic example of the application of civil forfeiture to gambling is the recent Reuben/Linda lottery investigation conducted by the Chicago police and the U. S. Attorney's Office. In this investigation, seven homes, a condominium, an eight-unit apartment building and a liquor store were seized for facilitating a multimillion-dollar illegal

50

lottery. Each of the offenses predicating the seizures in the Reuben/Linda investigation resulted in the arrest of the owner of the property and the recovery of more than $200,000 in wagers and other incriminating evidence. These seizures were in addition to more than 40 arrests, on 26 separate occasions, for violation of Illinois state gambling laws.

Lotteries are as old as America itself. Henry Chafetz (1960) notes that a lottery was used to help finance the Revolutionary War. During the 19th century, lotteries sponsored under state license were found throughout the United States. It was not until 1890, when problems surrounded the Louisiana Lottery, that Congress enacted legislation limiting lotteries by precluding them from using the United States mail. This prohibition, according to Abadinsky (1985), opened the way for the illegal lottery in the form of numbers and policy.

In numbers and policy a player selects one, two or three digit numbers from zero to nine and places a bet upon them. There are several schemes for determining the winning numbers including daily and weekly drawings, tabulating the results of the first three races at a local racetrack and using the results of legal state-run lotteries.

During the 1960s and 1970s, states faced with increasing budget demands looked to the lottery to supply badly needed revenue. It was also thought that the legalization of the lottery would deprive organized crime of a valuable source of income. Policy, numbers and bolita, its Latin American equivalent, have long been tied to traditional organized crime. Lawmakers hoped that state control of lottery gambling would divert funds from the underworld to such worthy causes as education. During the early history of the nation, many of the finest institutions of higher learning were in fact supported through the use of lotteries. Chafetz (1960) notes that Brown, Columbia, Yale and Harvard Universities all sponsored lotteries to supplement their budgets.

Though state lotteries have been successful in raising money, their impact upon organized crime is unclear. Susan Sharp, director of the Illinois State Lottery, states that an estimated $2.8 billion is spent each year on illegal lotteries nationwide (Tribune, 1989). She estimates that in Illinois alone, the Reuben/Linda lottery has deprived the state of $18 million in the six years that it has been known to exist. In Illinois, lottery revenue is used to fund the educational system. For each dollar spent in the Illinois lottery, the state education fund receives 41 cents. This so-called victimless crime has, therefore, deprived Illinois schoolchildren of $7.38 million.

The investigation of the Reuben/Linda lottery began in 1988 when Chicago police began piecing together information from various lottery arrests. Evidence revealed that bookies were hired to work in bars, restaurants, barber shops and other key locations to take bets ranging from 25 cents to $50 on the Illinois daily lottery. These bets were called into locations where teams of up to eight people would take the wagers. These conversations were even tape-recorded to resolve possible future disputes. Heavily played numbers were "laid off" through the purchase of thousands of dollars worth of legitimate Illinois State Lottery tickets. Finally, the records of the bets were delivered to the heads of the gambling organization.

One may ask why an individual would play an illegal game when they could effectively gamble in the same manner with the legal lottery. The answer is simple. The illegal lottery pays more. In the illegal lottery, you can play on credit and if you win there is no income tax. An advantage that the newer illegal lottery has over policy, numbers and bolita is that bettors can see the results displayed on television and printed in the newspapers unlike these older games where the results were occasionally rigged to cheat big winners.

The continued investigation into the Reuben/Linda lottery showed this organization to be very large and highly organized, employing dozens of workers in various capacities at a variety of locations in the Chicagoland area. These locations were used as centers for the collection and tabulation of wager information. At each of the locations raided by the Chicago police, officers routinely found multiple telephone lines, tape recordings of wagers, adding machines and betting slips reflecting thousands of dollars in wagers. For example, in the condominium owned by Reuben, Chicago police found seven telephone lines, six tape recorders, six calculators, and 30 cassettes containing $340,000 in tape-recorded bets.

During their search of a liquor store owned by Reuben, police uncovered telephone and utility bills for most of the "wire room" locations raided. Invoices were found reflecting the purchase of numerous calculators and other equipment of the type found in the searches of the wager collection centers. Personnel records were found for many of the gambling workers who had been arrested in the previous raids of the collection centers. Also recovered were thousands of Illinois State Lottery tickets that were purchased to "lay off" the heavily played lottery numbers. By purchasing large numbers of legitimate state lottery tickets, the managers of the Reuben/Linda lottery were able to reduce the amount that would have to be paid to the winners of a heavily played number should it be chosen. The more people who have a winning number the smaller the amount that would have to be paid.

As an indication of the high level of sophistication of this gambling organization, police found copies of formal rules setting forth regulations for operating hours, paid vacations, company loans and penalties for misrecorded bets. These rules also included prohibitions against talking back to supervisors and not keeping the work area clean. In one raid, officers recovered a payroll schedule listing 37 employees. A search of Reuben's luxury residence also uncovered gambling records, including "daily sheets" summarizing each day's gambling activity, and a large paper-shredding machine which was used to destroy the records of the bets. While officers were searching the Reuben residence, a runner for the organization arrived delivering a cassette tape containing betting records. A total of approximately $1.75 million in gambling wagers were recovered by the Chicago police in raids against the Reuben/Linda organization.

What is unique about the action taken against the Reuben/Linda lottery organization, and other similar forfeitures, is that the actions are civil in nature. It is not necessary to prove that the defendant committed a crime. The prosecution is against the property, not the defendant. Such forfeitures are based upon the "relation back" doctrine which vests title to property in the United States government as of the moment a criminal act is committed. At that instant all rights and legal title to the property pass to the government. Seizure and formal proceedings simply confirm the forfeiture that has already taken place.

They also provide owners with an opportunity to be heard as required by the due process clauses of the Fifth and Fourteenth Amendments to the Constitution.

Because of the relation back doctrine, the innocent owner of seized property traditionally has had no defense against its seizure. In other words, property whose owner was in no way responsible for its illegal use could still be forfeited. This position was upheld by the Supreme Court in 1974 by the Calero-Toledo v. Pearson Yacht Leasing Co. case (416 U.S. 663, 680). The origin of this harsh legal position is frequently traced to the Bible (Finklestein, 1973). Chapter 21 of the book of Exodus states:

> "If an ox gore a man or a woman, that they die, then the ox shall be surely stoned, and his flesh shall not be eaten; but the owner of the ox shall be quit."

The forfeiture of the ox does not depend on the guilt or innocence of the owner but only on the simple fact that the ox transgressed.

Innocent parties are, however, protected by remission procedures and in some instances by statute. Those who own or purchase property subject to forfeiture who do not have knowledge of the prohibited activity or tainted nature of the property may petition the government to pardon the property. The filing of a petition for remission of forfeiture does not deny that the property was involved in a violation of law but asks the attorney general to pardon the property because of the involvement of innocent parties.

Civil forfeiture actions are "in rem" proceedings against property that are used to determine ownership. This is in contrast to criminal forfeitures which are "in personam" and refer to actions directed against individuals to determine their obligations and liabilities. Unless a forfeiture statute expressly requires a conviction, it is considered a civil action against property, totally independent of any criminal action against anyone. Even an acquittal on the related criminal charge will not bar the civil forfeiture. Civil forfeiture differs from criminal forfeiture in that punishment is not the intention of the law. The purpose of civil forfeiture is to return property to its rightful owner. If Congress passes a law that makes all property used in violation of a statute forfeitable, once the crime is committed the property no longer belongs to the defendant but to the government.

In the Reuben/Linda case, the property was seized upon the government's demonstration that there was probable cause to believe that the property was used in violation of the government's prohibition against establishing an illegal gambling business.

This probable cause is the same as probable cause used to effect an arrest. It exists when the facts and circumstances justify a person of reasonable caution to conclude that the property was used in violation of the law. A determination of probable cause is always necessary for the forfeiture of seized property. If the forfeiture is contested, the government must present sufficient facts and circumstances at trial to meet the probable cause standard. Though forfeiture proceedings are civil in form, they are quasi-criminal in nature. The exclusionary rule does apply and evidence obtained in violation of an individual's constitutional rights cannot be considered in establishing probable cause. The fact that there is illegally obtained evidence, however, does not preclude forfeiture of property if there is other sufficient evidence to prove the violation of law.

Once probable cause is established, the burden of proof in a civil forfeiture prosecution shifts to the defendant. He must demonstrate to the court by a preponderance of the evidence that the property is not subject to forfeiture. The court must simply decide whose position is probably true, the government's or the claimant's. This shift in the burden of proof diminishes the Fifth Amendment privilege against self-incrimination. In effect, a defendant cannot pursue his claim to seized property without explaining ownership of the property. One can readily see the value of this in cases where the property is being seized as the proceeds of some illegal act.

CONTROLLED SUBSTANCES ACT

While virtually unheard of a few years ago, the seizure of property for narcotic violations is now a common event in the war on drugs. What is not a common event is the seizure of property without the arrest of the offender. Yet the Controlled Substances Act clearly provides for such seizures if money or property are the proceeds of drug trafficking or are used to facilitate a narcotic crime.

The word "proceeds" refers to property derived from money directly exchanged for drugs: that is, the profits of drug trafficking. A classic example of a civil proceeds forfeiture is the recent Rufus Sims case in which Chicago police seized two luxury homes, an apartment building, a Rolls-Royce automobile and $389,000 in cash from a drug kingpin. This case is an important example of the power of civil sanctions against organized criminal groups, particularly considering the fact that the target was never arrested and only 23 grams of heroin were recovered.

The Sims investigation began when Chicago police confiscated heroin and 50 firearms, including machine guns, rifles, semiautomatic handguns and 10 hand grenades from his home. These firearms were reportedly purchased by Sims to protect his narcotic business. Also recovered were titles to four luxury automobiles including a 1987 Rolls-Royce, five safety deposit box keys and the title to another home with an inground swimming pool. According to information received by Chicago police, Sims was a major drug dealer who specialized in selling cocaine and heroin in $10 and $20 packets. Documents recovered in an earlier arrest of Sims, and analyzed by the F.B.I. laboratory, estimated that Sims was distributing $225,000 to $430,000 worth of narcotics a month.

Based upon this information, the Chicago police began a civil forfeiture investigation of the assets identified in the raid on the Sims residence. Shortly after identifying the origins of the recovered bank box keys, Chicago police learned that Sims had made appointments to drill open each of the safety deposit boxes. A subsequent interview of the informant, that provided the information upon which the original search warrant was based, revealed that Sims was known to conceal drug proceeds in area banks. Armed with this information, Chicago police began a surveillance of the first scheduled drilling and observed Sims' common-law wife, who had been arrested in the earlier raid, and Sims' mother arrive carrying a folded leather satchel. A short time later they were observed exiting the bank, barely able to carry the now full satchel.

Believing that the two women were removing drug proceeds from the bank, they were approached and questioned by Chicago police. As the police came forward, one of the women threw a small cloth bag to the ground. An examination of the bag revealed that it contained approximately $5,000 in small denominations. Both women denied ownership of the bag and the larger satchel that they were carrying. When asked what was in the larger satchel, Sims' common-law wife stated that if the contents were money it was not hers. The satchel was searched by the police and found to contain $113,553. This money was then seized as drug proceeds because of the totality of the circumstances.

Civil seizures, just as an arrest, are based upon probable cause. In the Sims case, Chicago police believed that the seized money was the proceeds of drug trafficking. This belief was based upon the following: information received from an informant that Sims kept drug money in local banks; all concerned, including Sims' mother, had arrests for narcotic violations; the suspicious scheduled drillings at five different banks; the denial of ownership of the $113,553; the lack of employment by the possessor and the fact that Sims' mother was on welfare; a positive alert on the money by a drug detector dog; and a signed statement by the mother that she had no knowledge of the source of the money.

As a result of the information, search warrants were obtained for the remaining bank boxes and on the following day an additional $218,941 was recovered. In all, currency totaling $339,304 was recovered from bank boxes for which keys had been kept at the Sims' residence. Among the financial papers also recovered in one of the bank boxes was a deed to a 14-unit apartment building.

The continued investigation also allowed Chicago police and F.B.I. agents to seize Sims' Rolls-Royce and two other luxury automobiles identified in the raid on his residence. A review of the sales records at the automobile dealer revealed that Sims paid $176,681 for the Rolls-Royce, of which $129,461 was paid in cash and the remainder from a trade-in of a 1981 Rolls. The dealer's records also revealed that Sims had purchased two Cadillacs, one for $57,000 and the other for $26,800. All totaled, Sims had purchased three automobiles worth more than $200,000 from this dealer in two years. An interview of the car salesman revealed that Sims had paid cash in small denominations for each of these autos. Not bad for a man who was unemployed and had not filed tax returns!

Also recovered in the search of the Sims residence were documents relating to the appraisal of a suburban home with an inground swimming pool. A title search showed that the residence was currently held in trust. An interview of the last owner of record revealed that he had sold the property to Sims for $230,000. The previous owner thought Sims strange in that he had brought $200,000 cash in small bills to the closing. An investigation of Sims' apartment building revealed that he and his mother had paid $185,772 for the building, $90,000 of which was paid immediately and the remaining $70,000 paid within one year of the closing. In addition, it was discovered that Sims had contracted $120,000 worth of work on the apartment building in two years of which he had paid $97,000 in cash. His total cash expenditure on this property came to $282,772.

The government is able to forfeit these monies and other assets using the net worth method of proof. In a typical net worth case, the government shows that a drug trafficker has acquired substantial assets but has no legitimate or tax-declared source of income that could account for the accumulated wealth. Because the burden of proof in a civil forfeiture case is upon the defendant, he must prove that seized property is not subject to forfeiture once the government demonstrates probable cause to believe that the property is the proceeds of an illegal drug exchange. The defendant must show, by a preponderance of the evidence, that the property was purchased with money not derived from narcotics traffic.

In a proceeds case, it is not necessary to trace assets to some specific illegal act. The courts have construed the proceeds provision in a manner that permits the tracing of wealth to general, as opposed to specific acts of, narcotic trafficking. The government need only show some connection or "nexus" between the defendant and the narcotics trade. This connection can be established through the use of circumstantial evidence. In the case of Rufus Sims, the nexus was established by hearsay informant information and the fact that heroin was recovered at his residence.

Facilitation of a narcotic crime, according to the controlled Substances Act, means that property is used to make a violation of law easier. It is not the intention of the law, however, to take property from people merely because an offense was committed on the premises. Courts have interpreted "facilitation" to mean a significant connection between the property and an offense. As such, it is used sparingly. It is federal policy to proceed only against real property that has been substantially used to facilitate a violation of law as opposed to a remote or incidental use of such property.

A substantial violation occurs when large quantities of narcotics are recovered such as multiple kilograms of heroin or cocaine. Large estates, farms and ranches have been forfeited for containing clandestine drug laboratories and aircraft landing strips used to transship planeloads of marijuana and other controlled substances. Substantial violations also occur when property is repeatedly used in violation of the Controlled Substance Act. For example, five buildings were seized from Melvin Clay, a known drug dealer, by Chicago police: three for facilitating the distribution of narcotics, and two as the proceeds of illegal drug sales. These seizures were based upon 40 documented instances of minor narcotic trafficking occurring on or about the five adjacent buildings during a two-year period.

The civil forfeiture investigation of these properties began when district police asked the Chicago Asset Forfeiture Unit to assist them in abating a persistent narcotic problem. A contingent of the Vice Lords street gang had taken possession of a number of buildings at the intersection of Willard Court and Augusta Boulevard in Chicago. The "Headquarters," as they called the area, was located on a dead-end street that backed-up to a railroad overpass. Access to this area was strictly controlled by the gang members. According to Chicago police records, narcotic trafficking had been going on at this location for approximately 15 years.

The forfeiture unit began its investigation of the Headquarters through a computer analysis of all crimes occurring at the concerned addresses in the previous two years. They were able to identify 20 narcotics arrests occurring in or adjacent to the five buildings controlled by Clay in the Headquarters area. These arrests were the result of "drop cases," search warrant raids and undercover buys by informants and police officers. All of these arrests were for small amounts of drugs, usually no more than one or two grams. Each of these unrelated incidents became part of the civil forfeiture case in that they documented the existence of narcotic trafficking on these properties and, due to their large number, showed how the property was used substantially to violate the law.

Because of the nature of forfeiture proceedings, such hearsay evidence as informant information is admissible. This is an often misunderstood practice. The confusion arises out of the nature of forfeiture cases. The law does not require the government to make a prima facie case for forfeiture but only a mere showing that probable cause exists to believe that the property is subject to forfeiture. Hearsay, therefore, is admissible as probable cause in forfeiture seizures just as it is admissible in showing probable cause for an arrest or other criminal search and seizure.

In order to prevent the remission of the property upon seizure under the innocent owner exception, it was necessary to establish a connection between Clay, as the owner of record, and narcotic activity. This was done in a number of ways. The first was through his arrest record which reflected a number of narcotic arrests. Because the trier of fact's standard in civil proceedings is the preponderance of the evidence and not proof beyond a reasonable doubt, it was not necessary for Clay to have been convicted of any of these offenses. The fact that he had been arrested for narcotic violations was sufficient to tie him to narcotic activity.

Clay was further tied to narcotic trafficking through an informant buy that was used to obtain probable cause for a search warrant. Though Clay was never arrested for this drug sale, the evidence was admissible to establish probable cause for seizure. It should be mentioned that because of civil discovery, all witnesses including informants are subject to deposition and, therefore, disclosure of their identity. One can readily see the problems that this could entail for informants. Clay was also tied to narcotic trafficking through his own statements. He once boasted to local police, who were astute enough to record his statements, that law enforcement activity was hurting his drug operations. Clay also taunted the officers by saying that he had bought the concerned buildings with the profits of his drug sales.

All of the above information was gathered by the forfeiture unit from existing police department records. Legally it was enough in and of itself to seize Clay's property. In order to gather current information on drug violations at the Headquarters properties and strengthen the case, forfeiture unit personnel began a five-day video surveillance of the location. During this time countless numbers of people were observed arriving and leaving the Clay properties. Twice each day, for a total of 10 times, Chicago police stopped one of these people and searched them for narcotics. Each time a one-gram packet of cocaine or heroin was recovered. Statements were also taken, from those willing to cooperate, about narcotic trafficking at the Headquarters location and Clay's involvement.

Clay maintained a real estate office in one of these buildings. Acting in an undercover capacity, Chicago police met with Clay and asked him about the ownership of property in the area. Clay walked the police officers down the street and pointed to each of the buildings that he owned. While Clay was escorting the officers around his neighborhood, a woman actually approached Clay and asked him where she could purchase drugs. Clay sent her down the block to meet with one of his workers. When police stated to Clay that the neighborhood looked dangerous, the boastful Clay told police not to worry because he controlled all of the activity in the area.

Civil forfeitures allow the government to impose sanctions against people that are beyond the reach of the criminal law as was demonstrated by the Melvin Clay investigation. Because of his self proclaimed position as a "general" in the Vice Lords street gang, Clay did not routinely handle drugs himself. This was left to gang members. Clay was the boss of the narcotic operation. He provided the drugs which were sold by his underlings and controlled the use of the profits. Some of these profits were used to buy property in the area which, because of its proximity to downtown Chicago, was becoming very valuable.

Many criminals, such as Clay, are never prosecuted because there is not enough admissible evidence to make a strong criminal case against them. Such people and their criminal activity can be attacked through the use of the forfeiture laws. Because the government's burden of proof in a civil forfeiture action is much less than in a criminal case, and the property owner's innocence is generally not a defense, the criminal who escapes prosecution can be penalized financially through a civil forfeiture action by divesting him of the proceeds of his illegal activity.

Civil forfeiture could also be used to sanction people who make their property available for criminal endeavors but who are not sufficiently involved in the criminal scheme to be seriously sanctioned. This was the case in the Reuben/Linda investigation. Though all were charged with gambling violations, their penalties are likely to be no more than probation. Only the heads of the organization are likely to be incarcerated for any period of time.

Civil forfeiture is a rapidly evolving area in the field of law enforcement that holds great promise in society's efforts against organized criminal activity. Though often criticized as being a draconian remedy, civil forfeiture has continually withstood constitutional challenges. The use of both civil and criminal forfeiture is expanding especially in the field of narcotic enforcement. Forfeiture is being extended to other offenses as well. For example, the state of Florida has already extended forfeiture to the proceeds of any criminal offense that are obtained under a pattern of racketeering. When planning an investigation of organized crime, remember the power of the civil side.

BIBLIOGRAPHY

Abadinsky, Howard *Organized Crime.* Chicago: Nelson Hall, 1985.

Chafetz Henry. *Play the Devil: A History of Gambling in the U.S. from 1492 to 1955.* New York: Clark N. Potter, 1990.

Blau, Robert and John Gorman "5 Buildings Seized in Drug Crackdown" *Chicago Tribune.* September 14, 1988.

Gorman, John "U.S. Moves in on Drug Suspect". *Chicago Tribune.* April 20, 1989.

Gorman, John "10 Properties Seized in Raids on Sites Tied to Illegal Lottery." *Chicago Tribune.* June 1, 1989.

Federal Bureau of Investigation. Forfeiture and Abandoned Property Manual Washington D.C.: Federal Bureau of Investigation, 1986.

Myers, Harry L. and Joseph Brzostowski. Drug Agent's Guide to Forfeiture of Assets. Drug Enforcement Administration. Washington D.C.: U.S. Government Printing Office, 1987.

National Association of Attorneys General. *The Use of Civil Remedies in Organized Crime Control.* Raleigh, North Carolina: National Association of Attorneys General, 1976.

President's Commission on Law Enforcement and the Administration of Justice. Task Force Report: Organized Crime Washington D.C.: U.S. Government Printing Office, 1967.

Smith, David B. *Prosecution and Defense of Forfeiture Cases.* New York: Matthew Bender and Co., 1986.

Valukas, Anton R. and Thomas P. Walsh. "Forfeiture: When Uncle Sam Says You Can't Take It With You." *Litigation* 14-2: 31-37, 1988.

ROBERT M. LOMBARDO

Robert M. Lombardo has been a member of the Chicago Police Department for the past 20 years. He received his B.A. from the University of Illinois at Chicago (UIC); M.A. from DePaul University, where his thesis was "Narcotic Use and the Criminal Career"; he is currently at UIC working on his Doctorate in Sociology titled "Organized Crime and the Defendant Neighborhood." He is the commanding officer for the Asset Forfeiture Unit at the Chicago Police Department. He is a graduate of the FBI Academy. He has also served with the organized crime division of the Illinois Bureau of Investigation, Metropolitan Enforcement Group (MEG) and the narcotics and organized crime divisions of the Chicago Police Department.

ORGANIZED CRIME IN THE CHICAGO AREA

Judith F. Dobkin

OVERVIEW

Chicago, the nation's second largest commercial center, has within its metropolitan area the strongest La Cosa Nostra (LCN) family outside of New York City. Its influence extends to Milwaukee and several major cities west of the Mississippi including Kansas City, Phoenix, Las Vegas, Los Angeles and San Diego. The Chicago LCN has been primarily noted for its independence, cohesiveness, ruthlessness, wealth and success.

The Chicago organized crime family, known locally as the "Outfit," is an organized criminal enterprise which consists of an upper echelon leadership core, a mid-level management referred to in Chicago as "street bosses" and the members of the Outfit who report directly to the street bosses. The size of the Chicago family has been loosely estimated to range between 120 and 150 members, with 500-1,000 "associates" who commit crimes for and share profits with the family's members.

BUSINESS-LIKE STRUCTURE

The leadership of the Chicago family may presently be in flux due to the recent death of Joseph Ferriola, whom intelligence sources had viewed as the new leader of the Outfit after the 1986 convictions of Joseph Aiuppa, John Cerone, Angelo LaPietra and Joseph Lombardo in the Las Vegas skim trial held in Kansas City. The longtime leader of the Chicago family was Joseph Aiuppa, who set policy as to the conduct of the family's business and was responsible for dealing with the other LCN families throughout the United States. The second in command, or "underboss," was John Philip Cerone. The former "boss" of the Chicago LCN family, Anthony Accardo, is now considered a senior consultant to the present leadership.

Prior to the Kansas City trial, reporting directly to Aiuppa and Cerone were the Chicago family's six street bosses, five of whom lived in Chicago or its suburbs. They were Vincent Solano, the deceased Joseph Ferriola, Angelo LaPietra, Joseph Lombardo, Alfred J. Pilotto, and in Rockford, Illinois, until his death, Frank Busoemi. All but Solano and, of course, Ferriola and Busoemi are now in jail. While

63

Ferriola's successor has not been identified, intelligence sources have some ideas as to whom it is; and of course, it is difficult to know the extent of control the others exert from prison.

However, the street boss structure remains the same. These bosses control criminal and racketeering activity, usually in a particular geographical area. For example, Solano controls the north side of Chicago and is President of Local 1 of the Laborers' International Union of North America. Ferriola was responsible for the west side of Chicago and certain of the northwest suburbs and Lake County, Illinois. LaPietra controlled the near south and southwest side of the city and Lombardo controlled the northwest side from Chicago's Metropolitan Correctional Center for a while after his conviction in United States v. Roy Williams in late 1982.

Pilotto was President of Local 5 of the Laborers' union and, prior to his conviction in Miami for labor racketeering, controlled Chicago Heights (incidentally, his brother Henry was until recently the Chicago Heights police chief), the southern suburbs, and Will County, Illinois. He was probably succeeded by Albert Tocco. However, Tocco is presently in jail awaiting racketeering charges.

Each street boss in turn controls a group of trusted workers who comprise what the Chicago LCN calls a "street crew," and they in turn handle the day-to-day criminal activity which includes, among other things, loansharking (juice), prostitution, extortion and all forms of gambling.

Although membership of the Chicago LCN may be composed primarily of Italians of Sicilian, Calabrese and Neapolitan origins, one of its trademarks has been its ability to work with and ultimately control organized criminal activity of other ethnic and racial groups. For decades, for example, it has controlled or "taxed" the Jewish-dominated gambling organizations on Chicago's north side and northern suburbs. Principally through the efforts of Ken Eto (now a protected federal witness) and his Japanese associates, it has organized and taxed at various times black and Latino numbers and other gambling organizations. The Chicago LCN appears to have established the same relationship with Chicago's large Greek community, and either owns or shares in the profits of numerous Greek gambling businesses.

The influence of other traditional organized criminal groups in the Chicago area appears to be nil. In recent years there has been considerable evidence that the Chicago family has closely cooperated with the Civella LCN family in Kansas City regarding the operation of the Teamsters Central States Pension Fund, but it is a measure of the unchallenged authority of the Chicago LCN that there is no indication that any other major criminal group has attempted, much less succeeded, in operating here.

Probably the most significant non-Italian criminal organization in northern Illinois is the Herrera family, which has totally dominated the importation and distribution of heroin since the mid-1970s, following the elimination of Turkey as the point of origin for morphine base and its replacement by Durango, Mexico, the Herreras' home. Huge quantities of marijuana and cocaine continue to flood into the Chicago area; however, there does not appear to be any significant area-wide organizations controlling the drugs' importation or distribution. There is also an upcoming group of Colombians connected to Cali, Colombia, who appear to be increasing their drug-dealing activities in Chicago.

AREAS OF ORGANIZED CRIMINAL ACTIVITY

Gambling, most notably sports bookmaking, continues to be the primary revenue-producer for the Chicago LCN. Football and basketball are the favored sports with limited action taken on hockey and baseball. Most sports books are controlled by "independents" who pay a monthly "tax" to various members of the Chicago LCN in order to be allowed to operate.

Organized gambling in Chicago has cycled from outright ownership and control by the Outfit of major sports books to extortion of monthly payments from independents - the current situation. Because the transition in the 1970s was relatively disorderly, a number of independents were able to function outside of Outfit control until the past few years. The Outfit leadership then apparently declared an "open season" on independent bookmakers who were not associated with an Outfit member and permitted members to "claim" independent bookmaking operations wherever they were found. The result, in many cases, has been an expansion outside of traditional geographical areas by the more aggressive LCN factions, particularly the one which had been controlled by Joseph Ferriola. In the past several years, his crew has expanded to control or tax gambling and other illegal activities in Lake County, Illinois, and has begun expansion into Lake County, Indiana. However, there are still a few LCN members who continue to own and operate large scale, sophisticated sports books.

Various LCN members also control or tax a wide variety of non-sports gambling operations, particularly Greek and Italian dice and card games, floating high-stakes poker games and casino operations in several Chicago suburbs. A single such poker game, properly operated, can net its operator as much as $250,000 per year. This form of gambling, because it requires a large number of bettors and therefore is

65

much more visible to law enforcement, requires and perpetuates police corruption. The areas where local law enforcement has been viewed as being corrupt -- Chicago Heights, Stone Park, and Melrose Park, unincorporated Cook County and Lake County, Illinois; East Chicago and Lake County, Indiana, as examples -- are the same areas where one finds casino operations and numerous card and dice games.

A gambling case prosecuted a few years ago involved a lieutenant of Joseph Solano, Joseph "Little Caesar" DiVarco. DiVarco was prosecuted, along with several underlings, for operating a large scale bookmaking business on the north side. It was estimated they accepted gross wages of $10 million per year.

At a sentencing hearing, Ken Eto testified as to DiVarco's organized crime ties. Eto ran some of the ethnic gambling organizations, paying street tax to the Outfit through Joseph Solano. Eto became a government witness after a murder attempt on his life and testified as to how Solano and DiVarco were involved in setting up the attempt. He was shot in the head three times and abandoned in a car. The two men who shot him were later found murdered in the trunk of their car. DiVarco received a 10-year sentence, the longest sentence for a gambling conviction ever given in the Northern District of Illinois. He was immediately jailed under the new Bail Act and died in prison; therefore, there was no fine and no appeal.

Loansharking in northern Illinois is clearly dominated by the Outfit. Initially, and still principally, an offshoot of gambling, loansharking spread to a wide variety of legitimate businesses. There have been occasional instances of LCN loansharks financing narcotics transactions, but there is no evidence that such loans occur regularly or have any real significance in terms of the area's narcotics trafficking.

Loansharking is exceedingly difficult to prosecute. Victims would rather sit in jail on contempt charges than testify against the loansharks. The most recent prosecutions for this crime were those of Arnold and Grieco.

Joseph Grieco and his co-defendant, Joseph Arnold, were convicted of obstruction of justice. They threatened and bribed one of their victims not to testify before a federal grand jury investigating their activities. They were each sentenced to five years imprisonment and fined $15,000. The evidence at trial and at the sentencing hearing demonstrated that Grieco operated a loan sharking scheme under the guise of a legitimate lending company named Majestic Eagle. The business was set up under Illinois law to make small business-type loans under the usury exception which places no ceiling on interest rates as long as the loan is used by the borrower for a "business purpose."

66

Grieco reported directly to Chicago's LCN west side group, which was headed by Joseph Ferriola and handled all extortionate "business loans" for both Ferriola's group and the group which was controlled by Angelo LaPietra. Arnold was a loanshark who reported to DiVarco.

In addition to illegal gambling and loansharking, organized criminal activity includes legalized gambling -- through illegal hidden ownership in Nevada hotel-casinos. As a direct result of the Chicago family's influence over the Teamsters Central States Pension Fund, hundreds of millions of dollars have been loaned to a variety of individuals and companies associated with the Chicago and other LCN families to build or purchase hotel-casinos in Las Vegas and other Nevada cities. These loans generated huge kickbacks for Teamsters' insiders, employment for a large number of syndicate associates in the hotels and casinos and the granting of "concessions," that is, permission to own businesses located in the hotels or to produce the reviews or entertainment sponsored by the hotels.

Most significantly, the quid pro quo for the loan was usually "points" or a hidden ownership percentage in the hotel-casino for the LCN family or families responsible for arranging the loans from the Pension Fund. The Chicago family was paid its share of profits from its casinos via the "skim" - cash diverted from the casino counting rooms and slot machine proceeds and couriered monthly to Chicago. Some part of the Chicago family's monthly take from the casinos was split with the Kansas City, Milwaukee and Cleveland LCN families for their aid in obtaining Teamster loans in the 1960s and early 1970s.

Because of their role in directing these huge real estate investments to Nevada, the Chicago LCN has achieved significant political leverage in the state. Most notably in 1979, then-Teamsters Vice President Roy Williams and Allen Dorfman (acting on behalf of Chicago LCN street boss Joseph Lombardo) were able to approach then-U.S. Senator Howard Cannon of Nevada, chairman of the Senate Commerce Committee, seeking his assistance in defeating legislation bitterly opposed by the Teamsters to deregulate the trucking industry. As the evidence in their trial demonstrated, Dorfman and Williams, because of Dorfman's prior relationship with Cannon, were quickly able to conclude an arrangement with the Senator: he would stall the passage of the legislation while the Teamsters arranged the sale to him of some Pension Fund-owned property in Las Vegas at a favorable price.

Although trucking deregulation subsequently passed with Cannon's support after Dorfman and the Teamsters were unable to obtain the property at the price promised to the Senator, the episode dramatically demonstrates the access and influence in Nevada politics which has flowed to the Chicago LCN and their Teamsters associates from their former control over the investment policies of the Central States Pension Fund. A significant example of the tight control and ruthlessness of the Chicago LCN is seen in the killing of Allen Dorfman, shortly before his sentencing.

The Chicago LCN derives the bulk of its income not from conducting illegal activities, but from collecting "street tax" or monthly protection payments from non-LCN members who operate illegal businesses. While extortionate collections from independent gambling operations remain the largest single income producer for the Chicago LCN, close behind in terms of revenues are their collections from Chicago area "chop shops," prostitution operations, pornographic bookstores and gay bars.

An important chop shop investigation of a few years ago conducted by the FBI and the Chicago Police Department was called Operation Chisel. The investigation outlined in detail the operations of two Chicago chop shops that were stealing cars to order for auto parts businesses in Illinois and a number of other states, removing and selling the untraceable sheet metal parts from the stolen cars and laundering their payments to the car thieves and their receipts from their out-of-state customers through cooperative local currency exchanges. The Chicago LCN completely controls or taxes all such operations in northern Illinois and northwestern Indiana. The investigation resulted in 28 convictions. In the past two years, a joint FBI and Illinois Secretary of State Police investigation has resulted in approximately 60 federal and local prosecutions of chop shop-related crimes.

A significant organized crime-connected prostitution investigation, Operation Safebet, spanned four years and involved an undercover credit card business operated by the FBI and IRS. It was learned that organized prostitution flourished in Chicago's suburbs and provided huge profits to the Outfit. Conducted through fronts, such as show lounges, massage parlors and "escort" services, prostitution, until 1984, could be paid for by credit cards and thus provided organized crime with yet another business to tax: the credit card service company. The company acted as an intermediary to process credit card slips from the prostitute's customers. Thus, the service disguised the true nature of the houses of prostitution from the legitimate credit card companies.

The FBI took over this credit card processing business from an "independent" crook who was being extorted by the Chicago LCN. The FBI operated it in an undercover capacity. Operation Safebet has thus far produced 22 indictments of 75 defendants and 57 convictions. Seven sheriff's police have been convicted. Other prosecutions involved several operators of prostitution bars.

One indictment involved a prostitution/escort service in which six defendants were convicted of RICO, ITAR and tax violations. That case also had significant forfeiture allegations; a year prior to indictment the FBI and IRS seized almost one-half million dollars from one defendant's safety deposit box. The operator of the escort service and her two LCN associates were sentenced to prison. Two pieces of real estate and three personal computers which were used in the business were ordered forfeited.

Labor racketeering is another area of strength for the Outfit. Union corruption remains unchecked in Chicago and, with the possible exception of the Teamsters Central States Pension and Health and Welfare Funds, the picture today is little improved from 10 or 20 years ago. Members and associates of the Chicago LCN continue to occupy high offices in international unions with affiliates in the Chicago area and to control or affect the national policies of the International Brotherhood of Teamsters, the Laborers' International Union of North America and the Hotel and Restaurant Employees and Bartenders Union.

The International Brotherhood of Teamsters has long been one of the mainstays of the Chicago LCN, which controls or significantly influences a number of Chicago locals, according to FBI and Department of Labor intelligence. Although the International Brotherhood of Teamsters has unionized a wide variety of trades, organized crime influence is most marked in the trucking and warehousing industries.

Historically the businesses organized or threatened with organizing by the Teamsters have been susceptible to extortion to insure labor peace, extraction of bribes for sweetheart contracts and the extortionate imposition of goods and services supplied by mob-controlled businesses. The Teamsters locals have also provided the members of the Chicago LCN with union positions and legitimate sources of income.

The federal government seems to have been effective in ending organized crime's control over the multi-billion dollar Teamsters Central States Pension Fund by imposing independent management over the Fund's assets; however, the lessons learned by organized crime from the years of LCN control of the Central States Health and Welfare Fund continue to be applied in Chicago and nationwide. Modeled after the insurance services operations of Allen Dorfman, LCN-controlled medical, dental and vision care clinics and health care claims processing companies are now servicing a wide variety of union health and welfare funds in the Midwest, particularly from the Teamsters, Laborers' and Hotel and Restaurant Employees Unions. Such businesses typically are paid inflated fees for providing their services, receive kickbacks from the doctors, dentists and other professionals on their payrolls, provide medical and other health care services to mobsters and their associates free of charge and may "skim" from the funds by processing fraudulent claims. A case involving such allegations is presently awaiting trial in San Francisco.

Additionally, through the Teamsters' strength in the trucking industry in Chicago, it appears that the Chicago LCN can effectively control a number of Chicago's wholesale markets, most notably the produce market on the near west side. Because the control of transportation of perishable commodities effectively results in control of the industry locally, the extortion of non-union truck drivers making deliveries to the markets, as well as shakedowns of the wholesale produce houses and produce customers, is endemic; and it is widely accepted as the cost of doing business in these markets.

In hearings before Congress in the late 1970s, Justice Department officials identified the IBT, the Laborers' International Union of North America, the Hotel and Restaurant Employees and Bartenders Union and the Longshoremen's Union as being significantly infiltrated by organized crime. In particular, the Chicago faction was found to be in control of the IBT, the Laborers' union and the Hotel and Restaurant Employees Union. Several past presidents of the IBT have been indicted and convicted as has Alfred Pilotto, former president of Local 5 and International Vice President of the Laborers' union, who was convicted in Miami for labor racketeering.

While examples of LCN hidden ownership of legitimate businesses are legion, there does not appear to be any single industry which is owned or controlled by organized crime. Often attracted to businesses producing significant cash flows that permit the easy skimming of untaxed profits and the melding into legitimate profits of cash obtained from illegal businesses, Chicago LCN members and their associates are heavily involved in consumer credit operations, currency exchanges, vending and amusement machine leasing and repair, intra-city trucking, warehousing, restaurants, bars, show lounges, travel agencies, auto salvage yards and parts dealerships, garbage and industrial waste collection services, construction firms and discount stores. As noted previously, there is a significant concentration of LCN influence in the insurance and insurance services industry, particularly as they interface with union pension and health and welfare plans. These businesses are often run legitimately, inconspicuously producing "reportable" income or laundering monies obtained from illegal sources; they are often operated illegally as well, fronting for loansharking operations, extorting businesses from their legitimate customers and using violence against competitors.

Narcotics activity appears to be concentrated in wide-spread involvement by lower echelon Chicago LCN figures in mid-level cocaine trafficking and occasional instances of major importing activities. However, there is little, if any, evidence that the Chicago family is involved institutionally in any form of drug importation, processing or distribution. Importation and sale of heroin has been almost exclusively the province of Chicago's Mexican community since the mid-1970s, and there has been no evidence that traditional organized crime has any role in its sale. Like gambling, the sale of drugs, primarily cocaine, is just one of the many illegal options open to organized crime figures in the Chicago area.

The most significant new trend is seen in the Chinese organized crime groups bringing in heroin from Southeast Asia. DEA has estimated that over half the heroin in New York is from Asia. Several individuals are presently under indictment in Chicago for cocaine distribution and in New York for heroin distribution. The indictments were developed after a 1 1/2-year investigation that culminated in the seizure of over 835 pounds of high quality heroin and $3 million in cash in New York City in February 1989. Proceeding the seizure, two kilograms of cocaine were purchased by a cooperating witness in Chicago and 25 kilograms were seized in Detroit in July 1988.

Organized theft rings, hijacking and fencing are also part of organized crime business. The Chicago area has a number of organizations or "crews" of thieves operating under the control of an LCN member who selects their targets and is responsible for fencing the proceeds. The crews range from groups of extremely sophisticated burglars who specialize in alarm circumvention and who target jewelry stores, precious metals dealers and, occasionally, armored cars, to gangs of home invaders who concentrate on residential robberies and burglaries. It has long been believed that the upper echelon of the Chicago family receives a percentage of any significant armed robbery or burglary committed in the area.

Similarly, for years, the Chicago LCN has been heavily involved in the hijacking from trucking yards of semi-trailer loads of consumer electronics, cameras, cigarettes and other easily disposable items. Although the incidence of such hijacking appears to be down from the 1970s, there is no reason to doubt that such crimes remain targets of

71

opportunity for organized crime, which can easily warehouse and subsequently fence entire truckloads of stolen goods.

Public corruption provides organized crime with another area of activity. One of the principal mainstays of the Chicago family has been its political influence and control over various Chicago Democratic ward organizations and township and city governments in the suburbs. Aside from its traditional power in the ethnic Italian areas of the city and among organized labor, the Chicago LCN continues to maintain substantial political control in suburbs such as Melrose Park, Stone Park, Elmwood Park, Chicago Heights and Cicero, Illinois.

Equally important to the success of organized crime in Chicago has been the judicial and police corruption endemic to Chicago and the surrounding counties. Although the Chicago family hardly deserves credit for the pervasiveness of police shakedowns and payoffs, particularly of area bars, gambling operations and houses of prostitution, it remains the most significant beneficiary.

As previously mentioned, during Operation Safebet, for example, it was discovered that much of the Vice Unit of the Cook County Sheriff's Department had been receiving regular payments from owners of brothels in unincorporated Cook County in return for protecting their operations.

Some inroad into rooting out such corruption is being made. The recent "Greylord" investigation and prosecution of many local judges and lawyers has had an impact in the local judicial system.

Northwestern Indiana organized crime activities, principally in Lake County where the cities of Gary, Hammond and East Chicago are located, have been for the past 50 years and continue to be controlled by the Chicago organized crime family.

It appears that the Outfit does not own or control criminal activities in northwest Indiana. Rather, as in Chicago, they exact "street tax" or protection payments from most illegal businesses. The evidence is overwhelming that all sport books, numbers and bolita operations, and illegal slot and poker machines operators pay a monthly tax to the Outfit.

There is also substantial evidence that all chop shop and stolen auto activity in northwest Indiana has been for some time under the thumb of the Chicago family.

The Milwaukee, Wisconsin, area LCN family had been headed by Frank Balistrieri since the early 1960s, when his father-in-law, John Alioto, stepped down. According to the FBI, Alioto had been selected to run the Milwaukee family by Anthony Accardo. Balistrieri has since maintained a close alignment with the Chicago LCN and Accardo and Joseph Aiuppa.

Balistrieri's underboss was Steve J. DiSalvo, who acted as a "street boss" and enforcer for Balistrieri's various operations. Balistrieri and DiSalvo are presently incarcerated after being convicted in 1983 on charges stemming from their ownership of a sports bookmaking operation. Balistrieri was also convicted in 1984, together with his two lawyer sons Joseph and John Balistrieri, who are also in jail, for the attempted extortion of an FBI undercover vending machine business in Milwaukee. Frank Balistrieri was also convicted in 1986 in the Kansas City trial.

While Balistrieri owed his position to the Chicago Outfit, it appears that Milwaukee has always had its own organized crime family who consulted with Chicago only when matters involved organized crime people from outside of Milwaukee. Presently it is believed that the Milwaukee family is somewhat decimated. Two of Frank Balistrieri's henchmen who were on the rise, Anthony Pipito and Joseph Basile, have recently been convicted for conducting a large-scale cocaine distribution operation in the Milwaukee area.

The more things change, the more they remain the same: on one hand, a significant dent has been made in the leadership structure by putting high-level organized crime leaders in jail; on the other hand, greed is endemic and others will always be there to take their place.

JUDITH F. DOBKIN

In 1977 Judith Dobkin went with her Georgetown University law degree from prosecuting juveniles to mobsters by signing on with Department of Justice's Organized Crime and Racketeering section. At first based in Washington D.C. with the Strike Force and later in Chicago, she has an impressive history of federal court experience, including prosecution, advising, trial negotiations and appeals in a number of states, as well as the District of Columbia. In 1982, as a committee member of the American Bar Association's Criminal Justice Section, she participated in the development of the ABA's stand on the insanity defense.

Her legal experience has been in the area of economic crimes, involving tax, gambling, insurance, perjury and labor litigation.

In 1985 she testified before the President's Commission on Organized Crime and is currently an Advisory Board member of the Criminal Law Trial Practice Manual published by the Washington D.C. Bureau of National Affairs.

COMBATING ORGANIZED CRIME IN THE U.S.S.R.: Problems and Perspectives

Anatoli Volobuev

It is obvious that an urgent task for scientists and researchers everywhere is seeking the most efficient ways to counter organized crime, now that this phenomenon has become an international problem. That this problem is on the agenda of the forthcoming Eighth U.N. Congress on the Prevention of Crime and the Treatment of Offenders is indicative of the vital need for constant international cooperation and coordination.

Organized crime in the U.S.S.R. has received inadequate study abroad and, owing to peculiarities of social and economic development in the U.S.S.R., some propositions outlined here may be misunderstood.

Combating organized crime is one of the most urgent problems facing the U.S.S.R., and it is being widely discussed by lawyers, economists, psychologists and law enforcement officers. Since study of this problem began in the mid-1980s, many interpretations have arisen. This has been possible only in connection with the social reorientation of the U.S.S.R. (i.e., democratization and glasnost) and the consequent move to recognize openly the numerous negative phenomena that had actually existed in the country for many years.

This article represents the views of a group of researchers who have developed a concept of organized crime, its origin and progress.

The study adds to the foundation of the operational concept of organized crime. Researchers define organized crime as a relatively independent social phenomenon characterized by:

- the consolidation of criminal elements in a region or a country as a whole

- the division into hierarchical levels

- the formation of a group of leaders who are not implicated in the commission of specific crimes but who carry out organizational, administrative and ideological functions

- the involvement of corrupt officials in criminal activity
- the monopolization and extension of unlawful activity
- the creation of a counteraction system directed at the neutralization of all forms of social control

In order to add detail to this rather general definition, it is necessary to define particular features characterizing organized crime in the U.S.S.R. at this stage of its development. These features include:

- organizational and administrative structures, and their hierarchy, distinguishing the "higher echelon" members who exercise administrative and ideological functions not connected with specific crimes; they act with impunity since their actions are outside the framework of Soviet criminal law

- single norms of conduct and responsibility, or the specific system of norms, and values

- constant and planned character of unlawful activity, the common goals and the orientation to huge profits

- a system of planned neutralization of all forms of social control with the use of "intelligence" and "counter-intelligence:" the extraction of information relating to plans of actions of law enforcement agencies combating organized crime and the purposeful elaboration of countermeasures

- common funds invested in different spheres of criminal activity (which form the basis for the interlocking of common criminal and economic offenses) used for bribing important persons and for the financial support of the organized crime community

- monopolization and expansion of the spheres of criminal and other anti-social activity

- cooperation of organized criminal communities in different branches of the economy

- penetration of goods and services into the black market
- exploitation of narcobusiness, pornobusiness and prostitution
- creation and stabilization of the conditions favoring the deficit in the economy
- use of legal ways of "laundering" illegal profits
- active dissemination of criminal ideology, particularly in prisons
- moral and financial support of organized criminal community members serving their sentences and support of their families
- diversion of society's efforts from combating organized crime to dealing with minor problems

One cannot consider organized crime to be a sum of crimes committed by the organized criminal groups and professional criminals. It is a qualitatively new phenomenon.

A hypothetical model of the organized criminal community is presented as a pyramid. The base of the pyramid is the operative block, representing various dealers of underground business, organized criminal groupings (i.e., burglars, profiteers, swindlers), some professional criminals and those making unlawful profits.

Two more groups, the supply group and security group, are above the operative block. Above these is an elite group representing the intellectual center or leaders of the entire system.

The supply group consists of those who take no direct part in the commission of crimes. Their functions are implementation of the elite group directives; control over the activity of the operators; settlement of conflict between the criminal groupings and criminals composing the system's lower echelon; provision of stable communication between the organized criminal community and other similar organizations; security of the elite group members; provision of measures to increase the efficiency of operators' work; identification of other organized criminal groups, professional criminals and persons making unlawful profits and the inclusion of them into the system; propaganda and the dissemination of the criminal ideology; legalization of unlawfully obtained wealth; organization of financial and moral support for imprisoned community members and their families; and use of illicitly obtained profits to meet the personal needs of operators.

The security group includes persons helpful to the organized criminal community, for example, some corrupt officials (law enforcement agencies included), lawyers, physicians, journalists and those distinguished in the arts. Unwittingly they contribute to the higher efficiency of the organized criminal community's actions; provide social prestige to the higher echelon members; create conditions that impede efficient countermeasures against the criminal community; compromise or neutralize various social control or law enforcement officials actively countering organized crime; take measures to discharge the criminal community members from criminal responsibility or to mitigate punishment; assist in legal work; become familiar with law enforcement methods of combating crime; and provide operators with documents that can be falsified (i.e., medical or employment records).

This group's contacts with government representatives occupy a special place in its activity. The direct or indirect involvement of officials in organized crime activity is desirable in order to provide for the normal or safe functioning of the system on all levels, to serve not only as a security shield but to activate criminals, to open new perspectives for organized crime and to seize economic and political initiative. Therefore, close connections with corrupt officials is a basic feature of the system, which is why some experienced law enforcement officials define the Mafia as "politicized" crime.

In the system the "shadow" leaders (the elite group members) carry out the organizational, administrative and ideological functions. As a rule they have nothing to do with the commission of any crime, and are thus beyond the scope of Soviet criminal law. This makes their sphere of activity paracriminal. Their functions are crime control on the whole; searching for new spheres for criminal activity; development of measures aimed at the further monopolization of crime and other antisocial activity; adaptation of strategy and tactics of the organized criminal community depending on changing social and economic conditions; improvement of the standards and values of the criminal community system; and control over the supply and security group's activities.

It is necessary to point out that not only law enforcement officers but researchers believe that organized criminal communities have no strong vertical links but do have horizontal ones - interregional, local or republic-wide. The existence of an "intellectual center" of the organized crime system is debatable. At the same time, the lack of sufficient information on the vertical links cannot justify an optimistic outlook.

The system of organized crime pays much attention to labor and correctional institutions. There the leaders of the criminal community tackle such problems as the intensive dissemination of criminal ideology, exchange of information and recruitment of future "soldiers" of the Mafia.

At this point it is necessary to discuss the purpose of the upper echelons and why it is profitable for the low-level operators to merge into the system.

While at the initial stage the development of organized crime was marked by forcible expropriation of illegally acquired property, currently most operators consider it profitable to pay taxes to the top members voluntarily. The elite of the community then frees individual criminal groups, criminal-professionals and others from carrying out tedious organizational duties related to the commission of crime.

These duties include personal security and development of new techniques for the commission of crimes; legal and "illegal" defenses when a person bears criminal responsibility; the search for objects of infringement; the sale of criminally gained property; creating of opportunities for members of the criminal community to use their wealth in accordance with their personal needs and interests; guarantees of pecuniary aid in case of imprisonment, and the provision of employment for offenders after their release.

Thus, at present, the system of organized crime represents a "trade union" of sorts. However, belonging to a community of this kind includes not only voluntary membership (as in public trade unions), but also intimidation of resisting persons, because one of the urgent goals of organized crime is the monopolization of all spheres of its illegal activities.

At the same time it is necessary that members of the supply group exclude some operators, mainly non-criminal ones, from criminal activities. For example, it is impossible to impose a penalty on a person who provides the offender's family and the offender himself with pecuniary aid during the period of his imprisonment, who gives offenders an opportunity to earn spending money at restaurants or resorts and who finds an experienced lawyer for an upcoming trial.

When these operators contribute more directly to the successful commission of a crime, by performing preparatory work (for example, seeking an object for infringement, providing criminal operators with transportation or technical means) or by selling illicit property, they can be considered criminally liable for complicity in the crime but they are punishable by a less severe penalty compared to the punishment for direct involvement in a crime. It is difficult to impose a penalty on members of the supply group, because of the so-called "law of silence," which prevails among the criminal community of the U.S.S.R. At this time, it is not believed that the structure of organized crime in the U.S.S.R. is a criminal body with definitively developed and strictly defined functions. The organized criminal community is, in reality, not so precise. There is no doubt that the character of links between different components of organized crime is very complicated and the components themselves very diverse.

Depending on the special features of a region, organized crime can and must adapt to surrounding conditions. In various regions organized crime is at different stages of its development: from the initial racketeering to the fully-developed system defined not only by interlocking with general types of crime and economic crime but with official structural bodies.

As far as the structure of the organized criminal community is concerned, it is presumed that the development of this phenomenon necessitates its expansion to the national and international levels.

Some years ago, law enforcement agencies discovered some direct contacts of the organized crime leaders of the U.S.S.R. with their foreign colleagues. At present these contacts are constantly improving. It was noted at a KGB board meeting that "organizational links of smuggling groups and currency speculators with foreign criminal groups specializing in carrying out smuggling currency operations are being developed. The cases of illicit transit of batches of drugs across the territory of the Soviet Union as well as directly imported batches of drugs are increasing".

The use of contacts and other methods of carrying out organized crime exist. Recently evidence was obtained of Mafia operations disguised as legal commercial activities. The possibility of laundering "dirty money" is increasing due to investments in foreign banks.

The technically well-equipped Mafia hampers law enforcement efforts in combating crime. Criminals use modern foreign equipment, firearms, video techniques, radio communication, computers and the newest motor vehicles. Unfortunately, faced with this phenomenon, law enforcement agencies seem ill-prepared to combat these groups effectively. Reasons for this include the poor technical equipment of operative-investigative units of law enforcement agencies.

Successfully combating organized crime presupposes a fundamental re-evaluation of law enforcement strategy and a search for new forms and methods of operative-investigative activities. However, due to passive thinking and the tendency to follow accepted stereotypes, operative units usually counteract only the lower echelons of the Mafia, instituting criminal liability against its "unskilled workmen" - dealers and racketeers. These "soldiers" are immediately replaced by newly recruited "warriors."

The effectiveness of combating organized crime depends mostly on legislation. However, there is no reliable legal foundation for it in the U.S.S.R. which can be explained by the fact that the Fundamentals of Penal Legislation of the U.S.S.R. and the Fundamentals of Penal Procedures, as well as appropriate republican legislation, were adopted 30 years ago when there were neither political nor socio-economic prerequisites for organized crime. Reality has corrected these optimistic perspectives greatly.

At present, society is well aware of the menace of organized crime and complex measures are being undertaken to combat this evil. A national program to combat organized crime is being implemented. In this program the duties of all state agencies and public organizations will be determined.

On August 4, 1989, the Supreme Soviet of the U.S.S.R. adopted a resolution titled "The Reinforcement of Crime Combating Measures," which will greatly affect activities in this field. New penal legislation is now being prepared and it is hoped that the measures discussed here will be included in it. It would then be possible to combat successfully those in the upper echelons of organized crime, who are currently not punishable because their activities are beyond the limits of existing state criminal law. The new legislation should expand the jurisdiction of law enforcement agencies in combating organized crime and should create a reliable base of evidence against the guilty. It will be necessary to adopt a special All-Union Combating Organized Crime Law and to undertake other legal and organizational measures.

At present, the government is investing an enormous amount of funds to upgrade the technology available to law enforcement agencies. This investment will help to solve some problems and will contribute to raising the efficiency of relevant departments. In addition relationships between the Ministry of Internal Affairs, the KGB, the Procurator's Office and other law enforcement agencies are improving.

At the end of 1988 a special independent department for combating organized crime was created in the Ministry of Internal Affairs. Similar departments are now being created in republic and regional level law enforcement agencies.

No one believes it possible to eradicate organized crime in the near future, though the professionals do their utmost to provide tough controls over the Mafia and to create obstacles against spreading organized crime.

Realistically, the situation in the U.S.S.R. cannot be checked by measures applied at the national level. There are no state boundaries for organized crime and unfortunately the process of consolidation of the Mafia leaders from different countries is ahead of all prospects.

The U.S.S.R., therefore, fully supports the idea of the creation of an international instrument for counteracting organized crime and believes that the Soviet Union should take its appropriate place in it.

ANATOLI VOLOBUEV

Anatoli Volobuev was born in Moscow, U.S.S.R. He graduated from Moscow State University and holds the Candidate of Science Degree in law and also a Doctorate in Soviet Law. He is presently senior researcher with the Scientific Research Institute of the Ministry of Internal Affairs in Moscow. Dr. Volobuev has done research and published articles on the prison system in the Soviet Union and on organized crime. He is presently writing new legislation to deal with problems stemming from organized crime in his country.

MUNICIPAL CORRUPTION AND ORGANIZED CRIME

John Gardiner

Organized crime today shows up in many parts of the legitimate economy as well as many parts of the illegitimate economy. Over the last 30 to 40 years, it has become apparent that the influence and the costs of organized crime can be magnified by securing access to public officials, in order to either neutralize law enforcement or infiltrate the ways in which decisions are made, so that more parts of government become controlled enterprises. Chicago's Operation Greylord discovered widespread corruption within the judicial system, instances in which judges and their staffs, and the attorneys working in their courtrooms, exchanged extensive kickbacks to influence case decisions and the conduct of business within the court system.

The investigations in Chicago also uncovered situations in which the awarding of government contracts, whether for things as prosaic as fuel for the public transit buses or as exotic as computerized systems to collect parking tickets, was decided on the basis of the bribes offered to the decision-makers. This is not to argue that corruption always exists wherever you find organized crime, nor that the sphere of official corruption is identical to the sphere of organized crime; there are many, many forms of corruption that go beyond what is normally thought of as organized crime. The argument is a simple one: if we can understand the mechanisms that facilitate official corruption, it will enhance our ability to deal with the problems that law enforcement officials are dealing with, whether it be drugs or gambling or other activities.

It might be worthwhile to look beyond law enforcement or criminal justice approaches to the problems of official corruption. Certainly those tactics that have been developed by the strike forces, by the United States attorneys and other investigative groups to make cases and to establish sting operations are very efficient ways to collect intelligence to make cases where there is no direct cooperation of victims.

Beyond these criminal justice approaches are some mechanisms that deal with the unique problems of official corruption. One of the lessons learned over the last 20 years is that an ounce of prevention is worth a pound of cure. How can people in delicate situations be sensitized to the temptations they will face? How can training programs, for everyone from police recruits to experienced judges, infuse the wisdom to understand the situations that may be encountered, and give the strength or internal courage to say, "No, I want to be a professional, I am not going to participate in those kind of activities"? What is it that will strengthen everyone from an inspector enforcing a housing code, to a zoning administrator who is dealing with a multi-million dollar development application? The breadth of opportunities is enormous, and prevention programs must be as broad as those opportunities. In some cases, new legislation and codes of ethics have been created. Financial disclosure requirements have been instituted, so that more can be learned about the assets and liabilities of people in sensitive positions.

The inspector general programs developed in many federal government departments and in some states have taught the importance of systematic analysis of the ways in which government programs operate. As the opportunities available for perversion move from the traditional forms of vice, drugs, gambling and prostitution there is far more money to be made by bilking government programs than there is to be made in most traditional activities of organized crime. To understand who is abusing government programs, very sophisticated audit programs and investigations programs are required. Finally -- and this is a difficult fact for professional law enforcement people to accept -- it is necessary to directly confront the fact that many of those citizens for whom they work do not give a damn. For many people, the problems of corruption and the problems involved in organized crime and its many manifestations are either trivial or peripheral.

To deal with this problem, consider a spectacular program that has been operating in Hong Kong for the last five years. The Independent Commission Against Corruption is doing a wonderful job sensitizing the people of that community of five million to the dangers of organized crime, the dangers of corruption and the dangers of fraud against government. They are explicitly saying that public apathy may be the problem. Law enforcement officials ought to be talking with their governments about how to organize citizen education programs. The Chicago Crime Commission is regularly releasing reports to the citizens of Chicago about the nature of its crime problems and the problems of the criminal justice system. The Better Government Association in Chicago, another independent public service organization, also focuses on public education about the dangers of crooked officials. It is essential to tell citizens that the individual activities of a pusher or a gambling bookie are important problems that create significant costs for their community.

Finally, dealing with official corruption and other problems of fraud and abuse in government requires the designation of responsibility. Many organizations have very broad problems and very broad missions. Looking at their organization charts, *nobody* is responsible for dealing with the dangers of corruption. Police departments may be organized geographically, or in terms of particular types of crime, and may have no one responsible for the problem of official corruption, either within the department or within the community. The mission agencies, whether they sell housing or health services or transportation, in many cases also lack somebody whose responsibility is corruption. Law enforcement practitioners usually do not want to think about the possibility that their colleagues are selling them out; but unfortunately it may be weakening their ability to carry out their organizations' missions. The problem of corruption perhaps does not seem as significant as the problems of organized crime or the problems of terrorism . However, law enforcement practitioners should continue to focus their attention on it and they should try to persuade their communities to work on it as well.

JOHN A. GARDINER

John A. Gardiner, Ph.D., LL.B., is director of the Office of Social Science Research at the University of Illinois at Chicago. Admitted to the practice of law in Massachusetts and in the United States Supreme Court, he was a consultant to the Task Force on Organized Crime of the President's Commission on Law Enforcement and the Administration of Justice, and Research Director of the Chicago Ethics Project. He is the author of **The Politics of Corruption, Theft of the City: Corruption in America Politics, Decisions for Sale: Corruption in Zoning and Building Regulation,** *and* **The Fraud Control Game: Responses to Fraud in AFDC and Medicaid Programs.**

INTERPOL'S ROLE IN COMBATING ORGANIZED CRIME

Donald Lavey

Mafia, La Cosa Nostra, Camorra, Hell's Angels, Jamaican Posses, Colombian cocaine cartels and a host of other infamous criminal organizations are synonymous with corruption, murder, extortion, terror, manipulation and guile. They are the epitome of organized crime, involved in conscious, willful and long term activities and employing, within their own infrastructures, groups of persons practicing a division of labor and intending to commit criminal offenses. The aim of every organized criminal group is the realization of large financial profits as quickly as possible.

The problems caused by organized crime and organized criminal gangs no longer are confined to countries where criminal organizations are already well established. Indeed, the phenomenon has assumed disturbing proportions, and it is now widely recognized that networks of criminal gangs extend beyond national boundaries, exploiting ethnic, cultural and historic ties throughout the world. Organized criminal gangs have become increasingly more sophisticated, using profits, power and influence to insulate and protect their hierarchy from discovery and prosecution.

Financial profit is derived from every possible source of illegal activity, including traffic in securities, arms deals, smuggling, prostitution, gambling and, in particular, trafficking in and distribution of drugs. The phenomenon is so pervasive and deadly that its stranglehold affects virtually everyone in society today. The vast profits derived from criminal enterprise are being laundered through ostensibly legitimate businesses. Competition is eliminated by any means and the business strategy of such groups is the corruption of institutions, public officials and private citizens. Everyone is a victim. Corruption costs are inevitably passed on to the public sector, resulting in higher costs of consumer goods, inflated salaries and overpriced properties.

Traditionally, the picture conjured up by the use of the phrase "organized crime" equates with the so-called Italian crime families, with ties to labor racketeering, extortion, arson, narcotics and prostitution.

However, these groups no longer have a corner on crime. New groups have emerged and continue to emerge with new names and new schemes.

Outlaw motorcycle clubs such as the Hell's Angels, originally from California, have now developed international networks of chapters or branches around the world. Canada, Australia, Germany, France, Denmark, the Netherlands, United Kingdom, Austria and Switzerland all have chapters of the organization which retains its headquarters in Oakland, California. In addition to profit-oriented illegal activities such as the manufacture and distribution of methamphetamine, Hell's Angels have been known to shelter fugitives from one country in another. For example, in March 1988, a Hell's Angels member wanted for murder in Denmark was discovered in Canada; also in recent years, two Canadian Hell's Angels wanted for murder were arrested, one in the Netherlands and one in Germany. Both were extradited to Canada.

Names such as Triads, Yakuza and Jamaican Posses have infiltrated police jargon in recent years, and it is recognized that there are definite organizational patterns behind certain specialized criminal activities. However, not all so-called organized crime groups are as highly structured and regimented as the more traditional groups. Organizations can, perhaps, be categorized into four different groups.

The first group includes those Mafia-type families previously mentioned, where structured hierarchies, internal rules of discipline, codes of ethics and diversity in illegal and legitimate affairs are common practice. Outlaw motorcycle clubs, which may also exhibit a high degree of sophistication and diversity, are included in this category as are organizations such as the Colombian cocaine cartels. Generally, this group includes the largest and most developed types of criminal organizations that are implicated in a multiplicity of illicit activities.

The second group can be termed professional organizations. Professional because their members specialize in one or two specific illegal activities, although the organization may not be as structured as those previously mentioned. Such an organization would include operatives involved in car theft rings, clandestine drug laboratory operations and currency counterfeiters. Organized crime in this category would embrace those criminal organizations that are most numerous, and, although their spheres of operation are limited by comparison, their members are no less dedicated or dangerous.

The third classification of organized crime is probably the fastest growing type of criminal organization, with international repercussions, and includes all ethnic organized crime groups. It is difficult to state the exact reasons for the explosion of ethnic groups into organized crime. Possibly it is a result of a combination of circumstances such as the vast differences in living standards, overburdened immigration procedures and weak immigration laws.

Whatever the cause or causes, many immigrants simply merge into the criminal underworld, and, exploiting new and lucrative markets like opportunistic viruses, they avail themselves of contacts in their countries of origin to engage in narcotics and weapons trafficking, prostitution, gambling and vice. Using ethnic customs, backgrounds, fears and language, they are able to isolate and insulate themselves and to ensure their continued illegal operations. These same factors pose significant problems to effective law enforcement. Many immigrants have a dire fear and mistrust of police authorities and are reluctant to cooperate with officials in their adopted country. Foreign languages and close-knit ethnic communities make certain traditional police techniques such as undercover operations, physical surveillance and electronic eavesdropping difficult, if not impossible, to achieve.

This category not only includes the emergence of new ethnic gangs, but the territorial expansion of existing groups. It is unreasonable to single out one ethnic group: all have criminal elements as do their adopted countries' native populations. However, some cannot be overlooked.

Triads are secret Chinese criminal societies which predate European groups like the Camorra and Mafia by generations. They have their roots in the 17th century and were originally dedicated to the overthrow of a foreign dynasty. They have since developed into forceful criminal organizations with ties to Hong Kong and Taiwan and are actively engaged in the operation of illegal gambling casinos, loansharking, extortion and narcotics trafficking. Groups such as the 14 K and the San Yee On extend their control over Chinatowns throughout the world and have been known to collaborate with Cosa Nostra interests involved in narcotics trafficking.

Yakuza, (or Boryokudan), is a Japanese organized crime group composed of seven major gangs similar in composition to the Cosa Nostra. Within Japan they control the lucrative narcotics, prostitution, pornography and weapons trade. In Pacific coast states in America, they have been successful in generating unlimited capital by infiltrating legitimate businesses, such as hotels, condominiums and Japanese/American trading companies, and then extorting or skimming money. A Yakuza tactic called "sokiya", or corporate extortion, involves purchasing stock in a corporation and subsequently disrupting stockholder meetings through violence or filibustering until company officials pay them to desist.

Rastafarians are not just noted for reggae. Some members of this Jamaican group are involved in major criminal networks responsible for smuggling and marketing heroin, cocaine and marijuana, illicit weapons sales, credit card and airline ticket thefts and fraud and identification document fraud. Known as Posses in the U.S. and Yardies in the U.K., they are already well established in many aspects of criminal activity.

All ethnic gangs are legitimate focuses of law enforcement interest. All have a substantial deleterious impact on the ethnic communities since much of the crime will center on co-nationals. And, the general population will never remain unscathed as gang wars spill onto the streets, narcotics flood the community, extortion seeps into corporate boardrooms and corruption reaches the pockets of elected or appointed officials.

It is not suggested that ethnic criminal groups are responsible for all the crime occurring within communities. Nevertheless, criminal activities among certain alien groups have been well documented and are escalating at an alarming rate when measured by factors such as violent crimes committed and pervasiveness within communities. Because of unique daily contact with these ethnic groups, law enforcement has become increasingly aware of these criminal organizations and activities. Through new awareness and reorientation of priorities, law enforcement agencies have begun to place new emphasis on combating emerging organized ethnic criminal groups.

The final category of organized criminal gangs is rarely seen outside of certain law enforcement circles as organized crime at all; these groups are international terrorist organizations. Many countries have faced threats or demands from terrorist groups and some have experienced the horrifying results of refusal to negotiate with them. The origins of such terrorist actions are more often than not far removed from the jurisdiction of law enforcement in the country where the threat is levied. The solutions to such problems are also equally distant from the professional capabilities of many countries' law enforcement community.

That, too, was the case for Interpol where, until 1984, the major stumbling block in dealing with international terrorism had always been the prohibition on any involvement in political, military, religious or racial matters by virtue of Article 3 of Interpol's constitution and the political interpretation of terrorism. Indeed, the rather bland expression "violent crime by organized groups" euphemistically covered earlier assistance given in combating international terrorism, although assistance in combating aircraft hijacking and certain other forms of unlawful interference with civil aviation had been specifically allowed by a number of General Assembly resolutions since 1970. Spurred on, perhaps, by the progress made by other international conventions that did not admit exceptions for political reasons in extradition cases involving terrorist crimes (European Convention on the Suppression of Terrorism, Organization of American States Extradition Convention), Interpol itself took the important step of demystifying terrorism.

The 1984 General Assembly in Luxembourg passed a resolution asking that National Central Bureaus, while respecting the provisions of Article 3, cooperate as fully as possible to combat terrorism insofar as their national laws would permit. Furthermore, Article 3 was more closely defined to ensure minimal hindrance to this resolve. The strong consensus was to strip away the political trappings and to see terrorists as common criminals engaged in violent and bloody crime: terrorist acts, whether murder, hijacking or kidnapping, are treated as criminal acts regardless of the motivations or other underlying factors.

There are many other groups that can be placed in one of these four categories: the Sicilian Mafia, the Israeli Mafia, the Greek Mafia, Korean groups, Vietnamese organizations, Mexican narcotics cartels, Colombian and Marielito-Cuban cocaine rings, the Red Brigades, Tamil Tigers, the I.R.A.; they are all organized criminal gangs with significant international influence.

The activities associated with organized criminal groups take on an international aspect inasmuch as these activities, including traffic in securities, arms deals, smuggling and, in particular, trafficking and distribution of drugs, involve large numbers of personnel and vast distances between production sources, transit areas and consumer markets. Logistic support, intermediaries, systems of payment, profit accumulation and recycling methods require considerable financial resources and highly flexible organizational structures. Consequently as the amount of capital invested grows, the more the criminal organization's structure develops and the more pronounced the international aspect of its operation becomes. In addition, as capital investment increases, the more the organization will have to strengthen its structure by engaging in sophisticated forms of illicit activities.

Money laundering, undoubtedly, is a big international business with a varied clientele: drug dealers saddled with millions of dollars in cash per week; legitimate businessmen trying to evade taxes; giant corporations setting up slush funds for bribes and kickbacks; and ordinary people trying to hide their assets.

In the final analysis, crime that is aimed at making financial profit will occur and take root wherever criminals can operate successfully. And where they can operate successfully, it becomes obvious that they will make use of economic channels, in particular banking systems, which are designed to ensure the smooth flow of financial resources. It is in this field, perhaps, that law enforcement faces one of its most difficult problems, i.e., the tracing of proceeds and profits of illicit criminal activities. And it is also in this field that there is a need for greater international cooperation beyond the traditional area of strictly criminal matters.

One important inhibiting factor to law enforcement efforts in tackling international organized criminal gangs is the concept of traditional criminal laws, i.e., the one crime, one offender approach. However, since international criminal organizations handle crime like a multi-national business venture, the enormous division between the pretension of penal law and the reality of its enforcement must be recognized. The traditional legal approach is not sufficient in combating such organized criminal groups.

Mobility provided by 20th century transport, language barriers, modern banking facilities and technological advances in communications all create substantial difficulties for law enforcement in countering the activities of organized criminal gangs. Powerful and more penetrating legislation on a national basis and mutual assistance and cooperation on an international basis are essential tools in the fight against international organized crime.

The General Secretariat of Interpol is quite aware that these organized crime associations, both traditional and non-traditional, present one of the gravest challenges to the work of law enforcement officers. In this field the ability of Interpol to provide assistance to member states has been reassessed and adjustments have been made.

A major role undertaken by the General Secretariat has been through a cadre of dedicated and experienced police officers within its OC-FOPAC group, (Organized Crime - Fonds Provenant d'Activities Criminelles). This group places much of its emphasis on the financial side of criminal activities and the basic concept is that crime should not pay. As such, the group has become Interpol's pivot point in coordinating the implementation of new legislation aimed at hitting criminal organizations where it hurts - their wallets! Organized crime as a multi-faceted international business needs to be addressed from a global viewpoint, and the General Secretariat has been instrumental in the adoption by more than 20 countries of legislation to identify, trace, seize and sequester funds derived from illicit, ongoing criminal enterprise.

The realization of the need for this type of legislation is now gaining momentum and it has been recognized in Article 5 of *The New United*

Nations Convention Against Illicit Traffic in Narcotic Drugs and Psychotropic Substances, and in the work of *The Council of Europe's Select Committee of Experts on International Cooperation* in the drafting of a European Convention. The Secretariat will continue to monitor the use of such legislation and, in keeping abreast of amendments and new provisions, will advise and assist other member states with the introduction of related legislation in their respective countries.

Nevertheless, whether legislation is available or not, one of the greatest problems encountered in effectively addressing organized criminal groups is the reluctance or hesitation of government officials to recognize their very existence, or the extent of their impact on the community as a whole. Governments and police officials must learn from those nations that have had considerable experience in these areas and are achieving success.

Today, the power of organized crime reaches into every segment of society. It is a disease which leaves contaminated all that come in contact with it. It is an affront to every law-abiding citizen of the world. Now is the time for governments and law enforcement bodies to take notice and, more importantly, take action. Tomorrow may be too late!

DONALD LAVEY

Donald Lavey graduated from Notre Dame University in South Bend, Indiana, and received an M.A. degree in International Law and Relations from Catholic University in Washington, D.C. In 1972 he entered the Federal Bureau of Investigation as a Special Agent. He served in the field divisions in Cleveland, Akron, Detroit and Washington, D.C. from 1972 until 1981. From 1981 until 1984 he was assigned as Supervisory Special Agent in the Counter-Terrorism Section, FBI-Headquarters. From 1984 to 1986 he was assigned to the Legal Attache Office at the United States Embassy in Paris, France.

Mr. Lavey was nominated and then assigned as Chief of the newly-formed International Anti-Terrorism Unit at INTERPOL Headquarters, Saint Cloud, France, in October 1986, and now serves in that capacity at INTERPOL'S new Headquarters in Lyons, France. Mr. Lavey has worked counter-terrorism investigations for the Federal Bureau of Investigation since 1974, with a background in Middle Eastern investigations.

Currently, he is also an active member of the Terrorism Committee of the International Association of Chiefs of Police (IACP).

ORGANIZED CRIME IN AN INTERNATIONAL DIMENSION

Gennady Chebotarev

The intensive democratization of society has now made it possible to address the economic and socio-political problems facing the U.S.S.R. The silent avoidance of the problems in these areas and the indecisive formal measures of law enforcement agencies have left their mark on crime in society. Most importantly, they are expressed in the dangerous growth of professional and organized crime associated with corruption, bribery, extortion, narco-business and other illegal enterprises.

The importance of social reasons for the expansion of organized crime is obvious. Connected with this, the necessity for the development of wide-ranging government programs is optimal. To halt organized crime and suppress its appearance law enforcement agencies must initiate some realistic measures.

To give a complete and objective assessment of organized crime is not a simple task since it has, in many cases, a thoroughly masked character. Nevertheless, for the past three years its contours have been successfully mapped and an idea of its potential has been developed.

Some 3,000 established criminal groups have been uncovered, 20,000 active "authorities" of the criminal world have been identified, and more than 500 "thieves in the law," those who are the elite of the criminal world, have been identified. More than 200,000 thefts of government property and 16,000 cases of bribery have been reported. Property valued at approximately 350 million rubles has been seized and inventoried. Large interregional criminal groups have been discovered operating in the fields of transportation, gold mining, construction, trade, and fish and dairy and meat industries.

It is extremely difficult to identify the percentage of persons and goods diverted into organized crime using only court cases as an indicator. It is enough simply to say that measures taken so far have not shown signs of slowing the growth of organized crime. Short-term law enforcement campaigns and the use of random large-scale force cannot bring success against this growing dilemma.

In 1988 alone, the total losses from mercenary crimes reached 500 million rubles. Five thousand cases of bribery and 8,000 large-scale thefts were exposed. Approximately 300 kilograms of platinum, gold and silver and 2,000 carats of precious stones have been confiscated from thieves' dens. Group criminality has grown 38 percent. The number of so-called "dangerous recidivists," who have been committing crimes in groups, has increased 10.5 percent. Further consolidation of the criminal element is seen by the doubling of armed robberies and burglaries and by the rise in the number of unsolved professional crimes.

The activity of criminal groups is increasingly apparent in the economic sphere, linking the criminal world with various types of dealers and corrupt officials.

Practice shows that in many branches of the economy the bureaucratic structure of institutions and enterprises is frequently identical to the hierarchy of criminal groups in trade procurement, the service industry and the auto service industry. From 1986-88 in the Turkmen Republic, 34 established groups specializing in theft in the cotton industry were uncovered. The losses due to criminals amounted to approximately 31 million rubles. Among those indicted were 10 chairmen of collective farms and eight directors of cotton processing factories. Similar cases have been investigated in Uzbekistan and other republics.

Over the past two years in the Turkmen Republic in cases involving group crime, six workers of party and soviet agencies and 23 workers in the police have been dismissed and convicted. These workers, it turns out, were accomplices of organized crime groups.

The activities of groups which specialize in extortion of state, public, cooperative and personal property pose a serious danger to society. Cases of extortion have been noted in the theater and movie industry and among employees of bars, cafes and restaurants in the state sector in most major cities of the country. Estimates of the dynamics of the rackets are extremely disturbing even though they do not reflect the true dimensions of the problem. Twenty percent of all extortion in cities is committed by organized crime groups and, at the republic level, 50 percent.

It is quite evident that an intensive reorientation of the criminal element toward extortion is underway along with the consolidation and growth of criminal groups to an extent not accounted for in previous estimates. There has been a rise in the particularly dangerous formation of enforcers and body guards. The criminal acts they commit are marked by a particular boldness and cruelty which goes far beyond the bounds of the normal concept of criminality in the U.S.S.R.

The willingness to use weapons to demonstrate openly their power is characteristic of these groups. There have been several extremely dangerous gang shootouts in central areas of Moscow. More than 100 men have been involved in these fights over territory and spheres of influence. The use of massive force to suppress these excesses subjects bystanders and police officers to serious danger.

Analysis of this type of criminal activity demonstrates that it is frequently carried out on a high professional level. Attempts to persuade potential victims to cooperate in uncovering extortionists are rarely successful. In addition to the fear of physical reprisal and the destruction of property in cooperatives, people have been dissuaded from turning to the police. Instead they spend significant sums to bribe responsible officials in the areas of housing, food supply and other services. The concept of "official rackets" has already entered into the vocabulary of people involved in cooperative enterprises, and they consider it a more cruel and more significant infringement than the demands of the ordinary criminal element.

However, cases of uncovering corrupt officials are extremely rare. Unscrupulous cooperative owners and their protectors feel quite certain of themselves. There have been cases of covert extortion in which cooperatives are pressured into hiring members of criminal groups who receive salaries without working and with virtually no risk.

In view of the absence of the necessary legal rules for the protection of witnesses and victims of graft and blackmail, the use as evidence of data gathered in the course of an investigation and the use of modern technical means, proposals are being prepared to improve criminal law and criminal procedure law. It is hoped that the experience of countries that have already gone through the stage of convincing legislators to pass such laws will help the U.S.S.R. achieve this practical goal more quickly.

A specific problem in combatting organized crime appears to be the so-called "thieves in law." Their status as the top leaders of the criminal world and their position, from which they are given assistance from special monetary funds budgeted for "distinguished honors," can be traced to places of detention and incarceration.

During the period of unjustified repression, a period of extremely long prison terms, a period of brutal regimes and a period characterized by the de facto suspension of prisoners' rights, unwritten rules of internal regulation of colonies and camps and a defined structure of relations between convicted persons based on the dictates of the criminals themselves were formed.

In time, the ideology, mores and norms of behavior based on thieves' traditions were instituted outside places of incarceration also. All of this taken together gave rise to a phenomenon of power in the criminal world of the "authorities" who underwent a careful process of selection and a coronation within the milieu of leaders like themselves. They also hold honorable titles independent of their membership in one or another criminal group or clan. (A number of these criminals now reside in the United States.) Because they are bearers and active conductors of the thieves' ideology under the law of thieves, they influence the quality and the structure of professional crime which under defined conditions is growing into organized crime. In places of incarceration, the thieves actually play the role of a second government or a second administration, mediating conflicts, collecting taxes and distributing contraband goods within the colonies.

Of the 512 identified bosses at the present time, about one-half are free. Many of them have no permanent residence. They move constantly throughout the country and periodically hold meetings for the purpose of working out strategies and tactics of criminal activities. It is characteristic that approximately one-third of the thieves are from the Georgian Republic and, as a whole, the Caucasus region comprises 60 percent of this contingent. In connection with the recently observed modifications of the law of thieves, their adaptations to methods of contemporary social control have been noted. Twenty-five to 30 percent of them are falsely registered as workers. There has been a tendency to use them in mercenary activities of cooperatives. As a result, thieves' traditions have begun gradually to lose their significance. Their reorientation and discreditation has facilitated the growth of a new wave of criminal behavior which has other priorities.

It is very difficult to neutralize the influence of these criminals. As the experience of other countries has shown, passing special laws does not guarantee success. It is, therefore, necessary to learn about the practical work of the special departments of the police in other countries.

Under the current conditions in the U.S.S.R., the international aspect to organized crime has not been satisfactorily explored. Ending practices that limit departure from the country and significantly simplifying exit laws has sharply intensified the migration process and this has had implications for the criminal element too.

The new economic policy has facilitated the development of contacts among firms and businessmen and has led to the founding of joint enterprises and free economic zones.

Available materials demonstrate the active use of these processes by the criminal element. The police in the U.S.S.R. have obtained important data on currency operations involving counterfeit American dollars, data regarding the various channels of contraband narcotics and illegal operations involving works of art. The number of attempted skyjackings has increased as have other forms of terrorism.

There is serious evidence to suggest that significant forces of organized crime are very quickly reorienting themselves to crime with regard to foreigners who are presently being used as couriers from abroad. There is already a problem of guaranteeing the security of tourists from Poland whose accessibility has attracted groups of robbers on the highways.

Serious signals are given by the seizure of large amounts of hashish. It is hoped that the new policies of openness and glasnost introduced by the government will enable the U.S.S.R. law enforcement community to establish direct working relations with other police forces in the interest of common concerns.

GENNADY CHEBOTAREV

Gennady Chebotarev was born in the State of Turkmen in Central Asia. He was educated at the University of Turkmen and holds a degree in law. He began his police career as an inspector and then as a special criminal investigator, then became Chief Criminal Investigator.

For the past five years he has been a special officer for the M.V.D. dealing with theft of State and Public goods as well as with the theft of private property.

Mr. Chebotarev is now the Deputy Chief of the Special Section dealing with Organized Crime. Mr. Chebotarev holds the rank of Colonel.

AFRICAN-AMERICAN ORGANIZED CRIME: An Ignored Phenomenon

Frederick T. Martens

Abstract

The author examines African-American organized crime in both a historical and contemporary context. He contends that comparisons to Italian-American organized crime have resulted in a perceptual impairment on the part of those who argue black organized crime does not exist. Coupled with fears of being seen as racist as well as official apathy, African-American organized crime has escaped any serious examination. An examination of African-American organized crime may provide government with the knowledge to impede the spiraling disaffection of African-Americans with the economic and political mainstream of American society.

Few subjects evoke such an immediate emotional response as crime, and more particularly organized crime. Novels, autobiographies and movies continue to reinforce the ominous power and influence of the Mafia--a group of Italians who have been responsible, in part, for organizing crime in the United States and Italy. But to a large extent other ethnic and racial groups that have long been a part of the organized crime landscape in America have been ignored. Chin's recent book, *Chinese Subculture and Criminality* (1990), Dubro and Kaplan's *Yakuza* (1986), and Ianni's controversial *Black Mafia* (1974) have attempted to fill this void.

There is currently a justifiable concern about approaching the study of organized crime in ethnic or racial terms. Certainly, our experience with Italian-American organized crime demonstrates how misleading and damaging such treatment can be (Martens/Niederer, 1985). Nonetheless, the paucity of solid, credible research into these other forms of organized crime and their relationship to ethnicity and race is readily apparent[1], and given the growing evidence that significant changes have occurred in the underworld, it is a situation that should be remedied.

Law enforcement officials have repeatedly warned of "new" and emerging groups comprising Vietnamese, Colombians and Chinese that are filling the void created by the incarceration and deaths of Cosa Nostra members (P.S.I., 1988). Noticeably absent from these expressions of concern is any credible discussion about African-American organized crime. This may of course suggest that African-American organized crime does not exist, or it is not recognized or both. It may also suggest that potential discussants fear charges of racism. The truth perhaps partakes of all of these factors.

The Ambiguity of Defining Organized Crime

One of the great difficulties in discussing organized crime is the plethora of definitions of the term (Maltz 1990, 109-122; Blakey 1981). Organized crime has been defined simply as "two or more people engaged in crime." At the other end of the spectrum are elaborate definitions that describe complex organizational structures similar to those of a large multinational corporation (Cressey, 1969). An answer to this definitional malaise lies in Moore's (1987) "organizing assets"--criteria that are essential to organizing crime. For our purposes, it is better to describe organized crime than define it. Definitions are relatively inexact, perhaps too rigid and often far too ambiguous. What is perhaps more important is to describe the assets (Moore 1987) that organizing crime requires.

Violence or the Fear of Violence

Criminal markets require enforcement of rules, norms and territories through agreement with competing groups. Absent such agreements, or when these agreements are violated, the market will become

---

1   Ethnicity and race has become a recognized variable in treating illness. As Dr. Robert Murray of Howard University recently stated, "the idea of emphasizing ethnicity in medicine came up before...but it was downplayed because some felt the racial climate was too charged...Now people are beginning to say we have to address this because you get better results with your patients if you do" Leary C1. Would not the same analogy apply to the study of organized crime, the origins of which are traceable directly to culture?

disorganized. Violence will likely ensue in order to organize the market. Equally as important, the fear of violence may be sufficient to organize the market (Reuter 1982). What makes organized crime violence unique, however, is that it is selective, symbolic, and exacted for a distinct business or protective purpose.

Access to Political Institutions

The ability to corrupt is essential to the "peaceful" organization of crime. Public institutions, namely the police and the courts, are often used by the more adept racketeers to eliminate competition and exact "tribute." Moreover, through corrupt relationships with the police, dissidents and rule breakers can be sanctioned by the more adept racketeers (Furstenburg 1976; Dintino 1982; Faris 1989).

Control of and Access to Financial Assets

Access to financial institutions (e.g., banks, savings and loan associations, minority business grants, etc.) is another essential characteristic of an organized crime network. Those racketeers who can "lay their hands" on cash are more likely to corner a market than those who cannot. For example, the loanshark who can use the resources of a bank is in better position to exact market control than one without such access.

Experience

Success in any business is dependent upon experience, or more appropriately a unique expertise. Skill in bookmaking, narcotics trafficking, legitimate business investments, etc., will provide a distinct advantage over those who lack such skill.

By applying these assets to new and emerging criminal groups, it may be easier to gauge, with some degree of specificity and credibility, the likelihood of these groups posing a real, as opposed to a perceived, threat.

Superimposing the La Cosa Nostra Model on Organized Crime

In 1967, President Lyndon B. Johnson commissioned a task force on organized crime. With the assistance of four credible researchers--John Gardiner, G. Robert Blakey, Thomas Schelling and the late Donald Cressey--a report was issued that described the implications and consequences of organized crime on the body politic of society (*Task Force Report: Organized Crime*, 1967). It remains the classic piece on organized crime, and will be recognized as such for decades. The report focused primarily on Italian-American organized crime, and said nothing about other forms of organized crime. It did discuss organized crime from a broader theoretical perspective, however.

In 1976, the National Advisory Committee on Criminal Justice Standards and Goals once again examined the issue of organized crime. This body of authorities on organized crime attempted to shift the focus of organized crime from La Cosa Nostra (LCN), but were regrettably unsuccessful. According to the Advisory Committee,

Organized crime is not synonymous with the Mafia or La Cosa Nostra...The Mafia image is a common stereotype of organized crime members. Although a number of families of La Cosa Nostra are an important component of organized crime operations, they do not enjoy a monopoly on underworld activities. Today, a variety of groups is engaged in organized criminal activity (National Advisory Committee, 8).

The report however, failed to describe these groups, nor did it make any attempt to address the unique qualities of these other criminal groups.

In 1983, President Reagan, in what was to be a region-by-region analysis of organized crime, announced the formation of a Commission headed by Judge Irving Kaufman, a distinguished member of the Second Circuit Court of Appeals and the judge who tried the attendees of the now infamous Appalachian Conference in New York. Kaufman and the majority of this Commission remained at odds throughout the three years of the Commission's existence, issuing a final report that was ultimately rejected by 10 of the 19 remaining Commissioners. While this Commission made some respectable inroads into previously ignored areas of organized crime (e.g., corrupt attorneys and labor unions, money laundering, Colombian networks), it too failed to address African-American organized crime to any substantial degree.

The final report referred to the Black Guerrilla Family, which was, however, not organized crime in the pure sense of the term, but rather a political extremist group. This oversight occurred despite the fact that Leroy "Nicky" Barnes, a notorious black gangster in the seventies, outlined in his testimony before the Commission what was clearly an African-American crime syndicate. This omission, among others, prompted 10 of the 19 Commissioners to state, "The Commission...has failed to address the roles of American black and Jewish organizations in organized crime (President's Commission on Organized Crime 1985, 1986, 79, 177.)[2]

New York City Police Commissioner Lee Brown has been one of the few people to approach the issue of African-Americans and crime. Brown (1988) has addressed the volatile issue of street crime and drugs in the African-American community. Unfortunately, Brown makes no connection between African-American criminal syndicates, drugs and street crime. This inability to see organized crime from a broader perspective has obscured the variations and diversity that characterize the underworld. This situation is analogous to earlier refusals to accept La Cosa Nostra, despite the considerable evidence amassed to the contrary (Powers 1987; Schlessinger 1978).

What Should We Have Known About African-American Syndicates?

One need only research the literature to conclude as Smith did in 1971: there is more to organized crime than La Cosa Nostra. Haller, a most respected historian on organized crime, had devoted considerable research to ethnic specialization and organized crime (Haller, 1971-1972). In addressing the issue of blacks and organized crime, Haller stated,

There has, in fact, long been a close relationship of vice activities and Negro life in the cities...In the operation of entertainment facilities and policy rackets, black entrepreneurs found their major outlet and black politicians found their chief support (Haller, 221).

Lasswell and McKenna, in a pioneering study of the New York rackets, provided the 1983 Commission with what was certainly a probative document on black criminal syndicates (Lasswell and McKenna, 1972). They concluded that next to the federal government, numbers, an activity in which black syndicates were principally involved, was the largest employer in Bedford-Stuyvesant (New York). This study was conducted 11 years before the 1983 Organized Crime Commission, and four years before the 1976 Advisory Committee Report, yet it was cited in neither.

2   The Commission also ignored Jewish organized crime despite a book on this very topic writen in 1980, three years before the Commission began its work (Fried 1980)

In 1983, the New York City Police, in testimony before the Senate Judiciary Committee testified,

The American blacks have been employed within the Italian organized crime structure primarily at the lower levels of gambling operations in the inner-city areas...Many law enforcement agencies have come to recognize that black organized crime is growing into a distinct, clearly definable structure that must be dealt with in those terms (Senate Judiciary Committee, July 1983, 18-19).

The numbers racket was invented and controlled by blacks after World War I (Haller 1971; Light 1977).

Blacks maintained a predominant position in the gambling rackets, clearly superior to La Cosa Nostra. A "made" member of the Philadelphia LCN Family acknowledged that in 1929, when he initially began booking numbers in Philadelphia, he turned in his "action" to a black "banker" from Camden, New Jersey (H-79 Interview). In 1939, the policy rackets on Chicago's South Side were estimated to be an $18 million a-year industry, employing 5000 blacks. The stories of the late Madame St. Clair, Edward P. Jones, James Tooley, William "Woogie" Harris, and others clearly demonstrate the control of gambling exercised by black criminal syndicates, most of which were relied upon by political candidates for contributions, as well as protection (Hardy 1986).

After World War II, the picture changed dramatically. Jewish and Italian racketeers began to control the numbers rackets, using the police through corrupt politicians to raid black gambling operations. Extortionate demands were made of black racketeers, who ultimately succumbed to the political superiority of white racketeers. The late Representative Adam Clayton Powell, who represented Harlem, alleged that police were being used to aid the Italian-American crime syndicates in monopolizing the independent black lottery operations. Powell concluded that the police were targeting independent black rackets. He argued that "the Negro [should have] the same chance as the Italian" in the numbers racket (Powell 9).

Newark, New Jersey provides another example of this phenomenon. The late Mayor of Newark, Hugh Addonizio, was owned by LCN caporegime Ruggiero Boiardo. Boiardo was able to maintain a virtual monopoly over the numbers rackets in Newark, using the corrupt police to make raids on those who refused to pay "tribute" to "the mob." This ultimately resulted in a major race riot in 1967, as not only legitimate, but also illegitimate opportunities were closed to blacks (Lilley, 1968; Short, 1984).

Today, numbers is a declining source of relatively safe revenue to black gambling syndicates. State lotteries are effectively competing with the scarce but nonetheless always available gambling dollar in the black community. We are witnessing, however, a shift from gambling to narcotics--a far more lucrative, albeit riskier racket.

Contemporary Black Criminal Networks

In an earlier article, a point was made of the fact that African-Americans have used kinship as an organizing theme (Martens and Longfellow 1982, 3-8). This point directly refuted Ianni (1974) who concluded, "Among the Italian-Americans in organized crime these links were formed by the family and kinship system that dominate the culture...Among blacks and Hispanics the family seems less important (312). With respect to kinship, it is important to note that Leroy "Nicky" Barnes refers to an "oath of *brotherhood*" in testimony before the 1983 President's Crime Commission about a council of high level drug dealers (1983 Commission, 194-244). The Jeffers narcotics organization (1972) is referred to as "The Family" (Rudolph, 1); as is Bartlett's Philadelphia-based organization. The term "Black Mafia" was coined in Philadelphia in the early seventies (*The Inquirer*, September 17, 1974, 1); the organization headed by Frank Lucas, "The Country Boys," was a family in the blood-relative sense of the word (Taplin, 1975); and the emergence of an organization known as the "Junior Black Mafia" in Philadelphia, suggested a kinship relationship among its members analogous to Cosa Nostra, but perhaps not as powerful (e.g., junior). This desire to establish kinship as a bonding agent among these black criminal organizations is a technique used to instill loyalty and bonding among the members that transgresses routine or ordinary associations. It is not at all different from other legitimate groups, who often refer to themselves as brothers--fraternal, police, religious and union groups. It ensures, to the extent possible today, that a common bond unites the group, one based not only on a common goal, but more importantly, on a blood tie or kinship relationship.

Of further interest in attempting to explore the theme of kinship or family is the number of successful African-American racketeers who were born in the South and who organized their enterprises around the family. For example, Roland "Pops" Bartlett, a heroin trafficker who headed a heroin distribution network referred to as "The Family" and a successor of Tyrone Palmer's "Black Mafia," was born in Georgia (Caparella 1987). Frank Lucas and his brothers, Vernon Lee, Lee Van,

Larry and Ezell, were born in North Carolina (Taplin 1975); Frank Moten, a premier policy racketeer and loanshark, who was termed "The Black Godfather" by his criminal organization, was born in Thomasville, Georgia (Moten 1977); the legendary Frank Matthews, a fugitive from justice, was born in Durham, North Carolina; and the Chambers Brothers organization (e.g., Billie Jo, Larry, Otis and Willie Lee Chambers) originated in Marianna, Arkansas, and established a sophisticated drug network in Detroit, Michigan (Wilkerson, 1, 42) These common origins and the influence of the cultural mores of the South may be significant in several respects.

First, the notion of kinship as put forth by Ianni (1972, 1974) was perhaps no less strong in the agrarian South than it was in southern Italy, or in the Italian-American culture. In other words, the southern black family was just that, a family based on both a large extended family structure and a very tightly organized nuclear family. Oblinger (1978) seems to reinforce this conclusion,

From our findings, we get the feeling that what gave particular strength, endurance and shape to black culture and the feeling of community was the kin networks. Especially important were long-term obligations and reciprocal relationships in southern based communities based on these kin networks. I would even go so far as to say that there was an absolute interdependence [emphasis his] with kin when it came to feeding, clothing and sheltering families (22).

The organization of many of these black criminal networks relied upon the family unit as the bonding agent.

Second, the southern African-American has a rich history in the organization of people to achieve a common goal. The civil rights movement, which was a southern-born and southern-based movement, vividly demonstrated the ability of African-Americans to organize. This organizational ability was uniquely related to the southern experience, which relied upon both church and family to create a movement that changed the course of a nation.

Lastly, the rural work ethic, stressed individual initiative, and essentially attributed failure to the individual rather than the system. Thus, success as measured in American society by wealth, was a result of one's individual initiative, creativity and energy. This viewpoint is best illustrated in an interview with a 79-year-old black policy boss from Paterson, New Jersey, who was born in Georgia:

Well, a kid in the south, he lives with his mother. She's home, she feeds him, she shows him how to fry eggs, how to boil water. She shows him everything a home should have. The average kid in the north, he's too busy in the street, finding out what's happening. So he don't learn. Half the guys can't fry eggs...In the south, you count the ones who don't go to church. In the north, you count the ones that do go. That's the difference between the north and the south.

He articulated the values that were instilled in him as he was growing up in the North, careful to point out that these values were those of his parents (who were raised in the South).

I grew up in Englewood (New Jersey). We moved there when I was four years old. I moved in a white neighborhood, all Italians. Those same people are living there today. And if I went down the street and met Mrs. Gulliane, Mrs. Pecki, Mrs. Covini (phonetic), I had to say good morning or they would slap me behind the head. At night, at nine, ten, or eleven o'clock, and you were out and one of them asked you where you were going, son, you'd better tell them. Today, the kid is never wrong. We got kids here in Paterson, nine and ten that never have been in school a day (C-47, 1981).

Hence, the notion of family and kinship among the southern-born or-bred black suggests an organizational motif around which both legitimate and illegitimate networks are born, nurtured and perpetuated.

Loansharking and Legitimate Business

There is an inexplicable relationship between a mastery of gambling, loansharking and legitimate business entrepreneurship among African-American racketeers. Light was attuned to this relationship: "in many cases, numbers gamblers and loansharks are the same individuals...(and) have been the largest investors in black-owned business or ghetto real estate and the chief source of business capital in the ghetto real estate and the chief source of business capital in the ghetto" (Light 1977, 898).

In an analysis of 54 major black racketeers in the New York metropolitan area, the following findings emerged:

- Legitimate investment in businesses was noted among 84 percent of the violators mentioned.

- Business investments included restaurants, delicatessens, car washes, nightclubs, racing shops, automobile leasing companies, sporting goods stores, towing services, liquor stores, record shops, cab services, social clubs, cleaners, laundromats, stationery stores, grocery stores and apartments.

Among African-American racketeers, investment in legitimate business is an essential part of their illicit operations. The concept of individual entrepreneurship and ownership, sometimes using "fronts," is not at all alien to the African-American experience, particularly when contrasted with their past exclusion from government and certain sectors of the legitimate economy. The "mom and pop" store, the local "watering hole," or the various service businesses that populated black urban neighborhoods spoke well for the entrepreneurship of African-Americans. The case of Willie Price, an African-American racketeer, according to the Pennsylvania Crime Commission, is instructive on this point.

Willie Price, 56, is a racketeer in Chester, Pennsylvania. He was a boxer and had been involved in the killing of a black Muslim, who he claimed had broken into his home. He was involved in a small grocery business, in which he conducted his gambling and loansharking operations. He also financed his cousins, Philip and Warner Brooks, in narcotics operations.

A local folk hero, Price provided loans to local residents and workers at the local Penn Ship Yard. He "bankrolled" enterprising businesses in Chester and maintained a business partnership in a video poker and vending company with Joseph Iacona. Iacona was a close associate with Santo Idone, a "capo" in the Bruno/Scarfo LCN Family, who also maintained a gambling operation in Chester. Iacona was also in a business relationship with the former mayor of Chester, John Nacrelli, a convicted racketeer. The relationship of Price with both the political structure and the black community in Chester allowed him to exercise his power and influence in the illegitimate economy of Chester with no interference whatsoever from law enforcement.

Price skillfully built an enterprise that afforded him community support and protection, by reinvesting in the community. He represents a classic example of how African-American racketeers, much like their white counterparts, are able to apply business and organizational skills to the management of a criminal enterprise. Price also illustrates how "the rackets" are integrated into the social, political and economic fabric of a community. Successfully prosecuting and incapacitating Price, while certainly a necessary and worthwhile goal, would not alter the demands that must be met and are not being met by legitimate institutions (Pennsylvania Crime Commission 1988).

Differences Between African-American and Other Criminal Enterprises

There is an underlying belief among some in law enforcement and the research community that African-Americans lack the necessary assets to organize crime. Italian-Americans clearly possessed these assets, as did the Jewish before them and the Chinese and Colombians who have followed, these critics would argue. For example, the organizational structures of African-American enterprises do not exist distinct from the criminal activity they are engaged in, while La Cosa Nostra or the Bamboo Gang have an existence apart from their criminal activities. Nor is investment in legitimate business as extensive as among members of La Cosa Nostra, or the Japanese Yakuza. And certainly police corruption is not as pervasive as the early Italian-American crime syndicates found.

Inevitably, the comparison is made to crime syndicates with roots in centuries of tradition and culture, cultures that encouraged the emergence of secret societies. The African-American experience is far different, and is based on a different organizing motif. Furthermore, while we seem to be fixated to these bureaucratically and rigidly structured organizational models, that may be more fancy than fact. Credible research challenges the rigidity of these views and structures (Haller 1990; Reuter 1983; Block 1980; Chambliss 1978; Albini 1971; Smith 1975).

There has been little credible research conducted on the differences within what are perceived as relatively homogeneous criminal syndicates such as the Yakuza, La Cosa Nostra, and other criminal enterprises. We know so little about the organization of Colombian, Vietnamese, Chinese or Cuban criminal enterprises that comparisons and analyses are relatively meaningless. Even within La Cosa Nostra, virtually every family operates differently, with local exigencies often affecting both the model and the methods. La Cosa Nostra, the evidence seems to support, is not homogeneous in its structure or operations; geographic differences and variations do exist.

African-American criminal enterprises, many of which can trace their roots to the early numbers and policy rackets, represent the organization of crime. The organizing assets are clearly present: violence will be used when appropriate; corruption exists and is usually systemic; and there is access to financial resources, albeit via the loanshark. These enterprises may "lay off" to "mob-affiliated" or controlled banks, but they can and often do remain independent, so long as "political muscle" is not necessary. If "tribute" is exacted by La Cosa Nostra members, it is usually for "political muscle," a factor that is becoming less and less important today than in the past. While formal positions as "consigliere," "caporegime" and "soldier" do not dominate the lexicon of the African-American racketeer, there is little doubt among these racketeers who exercises what power.

The more stable and relatively safe "investments" in gambling are yielding to a new and relatively risky source of revenue--drugs. Here we are seeing criminal enterprises, some of which use family members and relatives and many of which do not, reshaping the African-American racketeer's landscape. The type of person attracted to this market may be and often is quite different from those who entered the numbers rackets. He or she is likely to be younger, less mature and more willing to resort to violence. Systemic avenues for corruption are less developed, and the likelihood of a successful prosecution is enhanced by the highly visible nature of the business, the immaturity of the participants and the expanding use of RICO.

African-American racketeers involved in the drug trade are certainly more vulnerable, but quite successful, providing success is measured in relatively large amounts of cash being generated over relatively short periods of time at a young age. Certainly Leroy "Nicky" Barnes, a multi-millionaire at the age of 40 (was featured on the cover of *The New York Times Magazine*), Tyrone Palmer, a millionaire at 24 (Faso, 3), and Garland Jeffers, who at 25 netted millions annually from heroin trafficking (Smothers, 12), represent that never-ending legion of African-American racketeers who sought a way out of the "chains of poverty" (Freeman 1986; Hughes 1988; Jaynes 1989). These criminal entrepreneurs, who were in fact "bosses" of large narcotics enterprises, represent a form of organized crime that has lacked any systematic, careful examination.

Prostitution rackets, loansharking and fencing are equally worthy of inquiry, for again we will uncover arrangements and accommodations between and among African-American racketeers that mirror what Haller (1990) and others are finding in studying La Cosa Nostra: criminal partnerships, in which the organization is often less important than the personal charisma of its leader or the money-making skills of the members.

African-Americans have a rich and compelling history of which "the rackets" are a part--but certainly not the overriding part. Our historical treatment of organized crime has been one of denial, skepticism, mystification, acceptance and over-reaction. Organized crime was perceived in its early years as nothing more than Italians killing or extorting from Italians. When its scope was finally acknowledged--some 40 years later--it was entrenched in the economic, political and social fabric of society. Italian-American organized crime was seen as the only form of organized crime and the hysteria that followed, while perhaps cathartic, was no less damaging to the Italian-American culture. Unfortunately, and regrettably, history is being repeated.

A Cautionary Concern

The recent prosecution of former Washington, D.C. mayor Marion Barry brought to the forefront an issue that underlies an apparent reluctance to confront African-American organized crime. The use of the criminal law as an oppressor of African-American and minority interests has taken currency in the last decade. There is certainly a perception that African-Americans suffer the effects of the criminal law disproportionately to others (Safire 1990; Zuckerman 1990; Krauthammer 1990, West 1990; *Sunday Star Ledger* 1990.).

Accenting and distinguishing African-American organized crime from other forms of organized crime only serves to advance the negative stereotypes and images currently prevalent in the media, law enforcement and society in general. This is a real concern and its implications are serious in terms of public policy. What then are the alternatives? Denial, conscious neglect, distortions, all of which will result in ill-founded public policy? Or creating a meaningful and accurate understanding of organized crime in the African-American community, which may begin to tell us something important about creating legitimate incentives to a rapidly increasing disenfranchised segment of society. Might we learn important lessons about organizing and mobilizing African-American communities, many of which are plagued with predatory crimes, by studying the organization of the rackets in the black community? Might we shed racist and ethnic prejudicial beliefs by recognizing the important and sometimes pivotal role racketeering plays in social mobility, assimilation and legitimacy in American society? Is it not intellectually dishonest to consciously ignore and disregard the functional role of the racketeer, whether of Asian, Italian or other origin in the economic, political and social lives of the disenfranchised? And might not government be more responsive to addressing the necessary incentives if we are to respond affirmatively and intelligently to the spiraling disaffection of young African-Americans?

Cynicism in government does nothing more than alienate an already disenfranchised segment of society. When racketeers serve as role models for youth, when hard-working, legitimate members of society are witness to the social, economic and political mobility of racketeers, and when government ignores and dismisses the reality of organized crime, regardless of its origins, the message is clear: money buys dignity.

NOTES

Albini, Joseph. 1971. *The American Mafia: Genesis of a Legend.* New York: Appleton-Century-Crofts.

Blakey, G.R., and Richard Billings. 1981. *The Plot to Kill the President.* New York: The Times Book.

Block, Alan. 1980. *East Side, West Side.* Cardiff, Wales: University College Press.

Brown, Lee P. 1988. "Crime in the Black Community." *State of Black America.* New York: National Urban League.

Caparella, Kitty. 1987. "The Big One: Raids Crack Roland Bartlett's Drug Empire." *Philadelphia Daily News*, March 17.

Chambliss, W. 1978. *On the Take.* Bloomington, Indiana: University of Indiana Press.

Chin, Ko-lin. 1990. *Chinese Subculture and Criminality.* New York: Greenwood Press.

Dintino, Justin J., and F.T. Martens. 1982. "The Process of Elimination." *Federal Probation.* Washington, D.C.: U.S. Government Printing Office.

Faso, F., and P. Meskil. 1974. "The New Mafia: Dope Dealing Fat Tyrone was Rich and Dead at 24." *Daily News* (N.Y.), June 10, June 14.

Ferretti, F. 1977. "Mister Untouchable." *The New York Times Magazine,* June 5.

Freeman, Richard B., and Harry J. Holzer. 1986. *The Black Youth Employment Crisis.* Chicago: University of Chicago Press.

Fried, Albert. 1980. *The Rise and Fall of the Jewish Gangster.* New York: Holt, Reinhardt.

Furstenberg, Mark. 1969. "Violence and Organized Crime." *Crimes of Violence.* Staff Report. Washington, D.C.: U.S. Government Printing Office.

Haller, M.H. 1971-72. "Organized Crime in Urban Society: Chicago in the Twentieth Century." *Journal of Social History.* (Winter).

_____ 1990. "Illegal Enterprise: A Theoretical and Historical Interpretation." *Criminology* 28 (2).

Hardy, C. 1986. *Vice, Crime and Violence During the Era of the Great Migration* (First Draft). Unpublished Paper, Department of History, Temple University, Philadelphia.

Hughes, M.A. 1988. *Poverty in America's Cities.* Washington, D.C.: National League of Cities.

Ianni, A.F.J. 1972. *A Family Business.* New York: Russell Sage Foundation.

_____ 1974. *Black Mafia.* New York: Simon and Schuster.

Jaynes, G. 1989. *A Common Destiny: Blacks in American Society.* Washington, D.C.: National Research Council.

Kaplan, D.E., and A. Dubro. 1986. *Yakuza.* Menlo Park, Calif.: Addison-Wesley Publishing Co.

Krauthammer, C. 1990. "The Black Rejectionist." *Time,* July 23.

Lasswell, H. and J. McKenna. 1972. *Organized Crime In An Inner Community.* Springfield, Va.: National Technical Information Service.

Leary, Warren E. 1990. "Uneasy Doctors Add Race-Consciousness to Diagnostic Tools." *The New York Times,* September 25, C 1, C 10.

Light, Ivan. 1977. "Numbers Gambling Among Blacks: A Financial Institution." *American Sociological Review* 42 (December)

Lilley, R. 1968. *A Report on the Civil Disorders In New Jersey.* Trenton, N.J.: State of New Jersey.

Maltz, M.D. 1990. *Measuring the Effectiveness of Organized Crime Control Efforts.* Chicago: University of Illinois at Chicago.

Martens, F.T., and C.M. Longfellow. 1982. "Shadows of Substance: Organized Crime Re-Considered." *Federal Probation* (December). Washington, D.C.: U.S. Government Printing Office.

_____ and M.C. Niederer. 1985. "Media Magic, Mafia Mania." *Federal Probation* (June).

Moore, Mark. 1987. *Major Issues in Organized Crime.* Washington, D.C.: National Institute of Justice.

Moten, Frank. 1977. "N.J. Drug Dealer Gets 25 Years." *Paterson Evening News.* Paterson, N.J. January 22.

National Advisory Committee on Criminal Justice Standards and Goals. 1976. *Organized Crime.* Washington, D.C.: U.S. Government Printing Office.

Newark Star Ledger. 1990. "Pattern of Racial 'Harassment' Seen in Prosecutions of Black Politicians." September 2, 30.

Oblinger, C. 1978. *Interviewing the People of Pennsylvania,* Harrisburg, Pa.: Pennsylvania Historical and Museum Commission.

Ohlin L. and R. Cloward. 1960. *Delinquency and Opportunity.* New York: Free Press.

Pennsylvania Crime Commission. 1988. *Racketeering In Chester, Pa.* Conshohocken, Pa.: Pennsylvania Crime Commission.

Permanent Subcommittee on Investigations 1988. *Organized Crime: 25 Years After Valachi.* Washington, D.C.: U.S. Government Printing Office. April 11, 15, 21, 22, 29.

Powell, A.C. 1960. "Powell Angry Over Arrests." *New York Times,* January 4, 9.

Powers, R.G. 1987. *Secrecy and Power: The Life of J. Edgar Hoover.* New York: The Free Press.

116

President's Commission on Law Enforcement and Administration of Justice. 1967. *Task Force Report: Organized Crime.* Washington, D.C.: U.S. Government Printing Office.

President's Commission on Organized Crime. 1985. *Organized Crime and Heroin Trafficking.* Washington, D.C.: U.S. Government Printing Office (February).

_____. 1986. *The Impact: Organized Crime Today.* April. Reuter, P. 1983. Disorganized Crime. Cambridge: MIT Press.

Rohter, L. 1990. "Black Panelists at N.A.A.C.P. Session Accuse Studios of Jewish Racism." *New York Times,* July 13, C5.

Rudolph, R. 1988. "W. Orange Man Held Without Bail as Leader of Large Jersey Drug Ring." *Newark Star Ledger,* 1.

Safire, W. 1990. "Unequal Justice." *New York Times,* August 14, A21.

Schlesinger, A.M. 1978. *Robert Kennedy and His Times.* New York: Ballentine Books.

Senate Judiciary Committee. U.S. Congress. 1983. *Organized Crime In the Northeast.* July 3.

Short, Martin. 1984. *Crime Inc.* London: Thames Methuen.

_____ 1989. Inside The Brotherhood. London: Grafton Books.

Smith, D.C., Jr. 1971. "Some Things That May Be More Important to Understand About Organized Crime Than Cosa Nostra." *University of Florida Law Review* 24 (no. 1).

_____ 1975. *The Mafia Mystique.* New York: Basic Books.

Smothers, D. 1972. "Gary, Indiana, The Family, The Godfather, and the Present Hush." *Paterson Evening News.* Paterson, N.J. December 4.

Taplin, C.R. 1975. "Lucas Family Troubles." *The Sunday Bergen Record.* Hackensack, N.J.

Task Force Report: Organized Crime. 1967. Washington, D.C.: U.S. Government Printing Office.

West, Diana. 1990. "Harsh Judgement of Black Racism." *Insight*. June, 18.

Wilkerson, I. 1988. "Detroit Drug Empire Showed All the Traits of Big Business." *New York Times,* December 18.

Zuckerman, M.B. 1990. "Mentioning the Unmentionable." *U.S. News and World Report,* June 4.

Interview of Confidential Source C-47. 1981. Paterson, New Jersey. October.

Interview of Confidential Source H-79. 1989. Pennsylvania. July.

FREDERICK T. MARTENS

Mr. Martens has served as the President of the International Association for the Study of Organized Crime, has received an award for his work on intelligence from the International Association of Intelligence Analysts, and has received commendations for outstanding police work with the New Jersey State Police. He has served as a consultant to the National Institute of Justice, New Scotland Yard, the Colorado Department of Public Safety, Koba Association, the Northwest Policy Studies Center, Thames Television (1981-83; 1990-present), and the Law Enforcement Accreditation Commission, where he evaluated the Florida Department of Law Enforcement.

Mr. Martens has devoted his career to the investigation of organized crime and narcotics. He has testified and been qualified as an expert on organized crime by the Pennsylvania Supreme Court, the Pennsylvania Commonwealth Court, the Permanent Sub-Committee on Investigations (PSI) and the Senate Judiciary Committee.

INDEX

23, 31-32, 91
in Canada 1-10
banks used in 4-5
brokerage houses used in 5
couriers used in 6
lawyers used in 7
money exchanges used in 5
offshore corporations used in 7
and repatriation techniques 8-9
travel agencies used in 6
in United Kingdom 31-32
U.S. News and World Report
article on 21
Moran, Richard 19, 27

Nevada 67
New Scotland Yard 30, 31, 32,
33, 34
Specialist Operations 32, 34
Task Squad 33-34
Newark, N.J, corruption in 106
Nuremburg Court 44

O'Bront, William 3
Operation Chisel 68
Operation Cougar 34-35
Operation Greylord 83
Operation Man 34-35
Operation Safebet 68-69, 72
Organized crime 50, 51, 87,
88-89, 91,92
African-American 101-117
asset forfeiture used against
47-60
in Canada 1-10
in Chicago 47-60, 63-73
defined 14-15, 29, 75-76, 102
and drug trafficking 14, 19-27,
65
and ethnic gangs 21-22, 64,
88-90, 91, 101, 111
and extortion 69, 96

and gambling 50, 64, 65-66,
67, 68
groups categorized 88-89
and illegal lotteries 51
in Indiana 72
and insurance business 70
Jewish 104
and loansharking 66-67
in Milwaukee 72-73
Prohibition, as impetus for
19, 20, 21-22
and prostitution 68-69
and protection payments 68
and public corruption 30, 66, 72,
83-85, 96, 102, 106
technology used by 15, 80
and theft 68, 71
in the United Kingdom 29-35
in the U.S.S.R. 75-82, 95, 99
Organized Crime,
African-American 101-117
contrasted with other crime
groups 110-111
and drug trafficking 111
and gambling 105-106, 109
groups 106-107
kinship ties, important of in
107-109
lack of research on 101-102
legitimate businesses involved
in 109
and numbers racket 105-106
Southern values seen as
influential in 107-109
Organized Crime Control Act of
1970 49, 50
"Outfit." See La Cosa Nostra, in
Chicago

Pilotto, Alfred J. 63, 64, 70
Pipito, Anthony 73
Police, U.K. 30, 31, 32-34

International perspectives
on organized crime